The path to fulfilling our God-given purpose is filled with numerous twists, turns, and challenges. In *Standing Strong*, Alli shows us how to press through our fears, doubts, and self-imposed limitations in order to embark on the exhilarating faith-filled adventure we are each destined to live. This book is full of wisdom, grace, and honesty. I loved it and know you will too.

CHRISTINE CAINE, FOUNDER OF A21 AND PROPEL WOMEN

Empowering and timely. Alli writes like the honest best friend who gives us the truth we crave coupled with the kick in the pants we need. Read this book!

JORDAN LEE DOOLEY, NATIONAL BESTSELLING AUTHOR OF *OWN YOUR EVERYDAY*

If you're tired of messaging that makes you feel subpar and not enough, *Standing Strong* is the antidote! Every chapter is a stepping-stone that leads women to stand on truth. Alli's words are more than a manual or a self-help guide; they teach us *how* to be the women God has called us to be. Her heart to help women is palpable in this book. This is not only a book, it's the core essence of what Alli believes and who she is!

BIANCA JUÁREZ OLTHOFF, SPEAKER, TEACHER, AND BESTSELLING AUTHOR OF *HOW TO HAVE YOUR LIFE NOT SUCK*

When you have to rise up from the ashes of your life or face a mountain range of challenges that discourage and intimidate you, you need someone to stand by your side, someone filled with empathy, clarity, and insight. Alli Worthington is your woman, and *Standing Strong* is the guide she has written for your journey. You see, Alli gets it. She has been there. So the truths she shares on these pages are truths she lives by, and she offers you wisdom hard-won in the trenches of her life. I've watched Alli stand strong in the face of adversity, and through this book she'll empower you to do the same.

JO SAXTON, LEADERSHIP COACH, PODCAST HOST, AND AUTHOR OF *READY TO RISE*

In a time when the world needs it the most, Alli's voice blazes a new call to partner with God for every little thing. With a confidence that comes only from living out the story firsthand, Alli boldly scraps the idea of hustling for our own worth and reminds us that we are called to abundance, not some meager sense of being "enough." Revisit this book every time you need a reminder that God is for you, he is fighting for you, and he is constantly calling you to live a brave life outside the lines while inside his power. Write these reminders on the walls of your heart.

HANNAH BRENCHER, AUTHOR, FOUNDER OF MORE LOVE LETTERS, AND ONLINE EDUCATOR

Standing Strong is the book I've been waiting for Alli Worthington to write! In a world that often exalts self-discovery, Alli never leaves out the required components of pushing through fear, fully trusting, and constantly depending on God. *Standing Strong* is a must-read for anyone looking for a Christ-centered guide to walking through change, transition, and transformation.

HAVILAH CUNNINGTON, AUTHOR OF *STRONGER THAN THE STRUGGLE*, FOUNDER OF TRUTH TO TABLE

In her book *Standing Strong*, Alli Worthington invites readers to engage in saying yes to God by pushing away the lies that hold them hostage so they can stand firm, move forward, and live purposefully as they were designed to do.

CHRYSTAL EVANS HURST, BESTSELLING AUTHOR AND SPEAKER

Forget pep talks—women need more than that. Packed with practical wisdom, *Standing Strong* is a word for this time. Alli Worthington holds the torch out front as our troop leader, guiding us to a place of overdue confidence in our faith and our call. I'm with her, all the way.

LISA WHITTLE, AUTHOR, PODCAST HOST, AND COFOUNDER OF CALLED CREATIVES

If your life has been plagued by self-doubt, by feelings of never being enough, Alli has given us a road map to saying yes to who God says we are.

SHEILA WALSH, AUTHOR OF *PRAYING WOMEN* AND *PRAYING GIRLS*

Standing Strong

Standing Strong

A WOMAN'S GUIDE TO OVERCOMING ADVERSITY
AND LIVING WITH CONFIDENCE

ALLI WORTHINGTON

ZONDERVAN
BOOKS

ZONDERVAN BOOKS

Standing Strong
Copyright © 2020 by Alli Worthington

Requests for information should be addressed to:
Zondervan, *3900 Sparks Dr. SE, Grand Rapids, Michigan 49546*

Zondervan titles may be purchased in bulk for educational, business, fundraising, or sales promotional use. For information, please email SpecialMarkets@Zondervan.com.

ISBN 978-0-310-35878-7 (audio)

Library of Congress Cataloging-in-Publication Data

Names: Worthington, Alli, author.
    Title: Standing strong : a woman's guide to overcoming adversity and living with confidence / Alli Worthington.
    Description: Grand Rapids : Zondervan, 2020. | Includes bibliographical references. | Summary: "Standing Strong by bestselling author Alli Worthington is an empowering guide to escaping the prison of your self-doubt and saying yes to God's calling instead"— Provided by publisher.
    Identifiers: LCCN 2020017006 (print) | LCCN 2020017007 (ebook) | ISBN 9780310358763 (trade paperback) | ISBN 9780310358770 (ebook)
    Subjects: LCSH: Christian women—Religious life. | Christian women—Conduct of life. | Women—Religious life.
    Classification: LCC BV4527 .W643 2020 (print) | LCC BV4527 (ebook) | DDC 248.8/43—dc23
    LC record available at https://lccn.loc.gov/2020017006
    LC ebook record available at https://lccn.loc.gov/2020017007

Published in association with literary agent Jenni Burke of Illuminate Literary Agency, www.illuminateliterary.com.

Cover design: James W. Hall IV
Cover photography: Hannah Capps Photography
Interior design: Emily Ghattas

Printed in the United States of America

20 21 22 23 24 /LSC/ 10 9 8 7 6 5 4 3 2 1

For my friends who stood by my side and kept me standing strong—Bianca, Carol, and Stephanie. I am forever grateful for your friendship, your willingness to speak truth to me even when I didn't want to hear it, and your belief in me when self-doubt threatened to take me out.

Contents

Part 3: How to Move Forward with Confidence

Standing Strong Manifesto

A strong woman is a surrounded woman. Not a got-it-all-together woman but a got-my-God-around-me woman. She's not just a gifted woman; she's a giving woman. A wonder woman. She steps in stride without striving because she's a learning, loving, letting go woman. She holds her head up high, even though life hits hard and swings low. She knows in her soul that she's never been alone—never left out, never ever put on hold. She lifts her hands, raising praise for endless days no matter the pain, no matter how the path gives way before her. A serving woman, born with palms up and hands stretched out toward others. She knows standing strong is standing long together—looks like locking arms and hearts together. She stands strong in the strength of the Holy One, the only one able to heal and hold her. Behold her bold, behold her brave, behold *her*. Standing strong—living and leading right where she belongs.

—RACHEL MARIE KANG

Part One

Say Yes and Amen to What God Has for You

To live into the woman God made you to be, you have to believe what God has said about you. And to accomplish what God has called you to do, you have to follow his lead—and never turn back.

Can you imagine a generation of women saying yes and amen to God? Imagine the confidence we would have. Imagine how it would transform our relationships, our families, and our communities. Imagine how we would change this world for the better.

This turbulent world, turned upside down by calamities, catastrophes, and contagions, is crying out for a generation of women who are daughters of the king, are filled with the Holy Spirit, and who get their strength from God to live in a way that matters.

The only way we do that is by making the decision to believe that what God says about us is true. Let's say yes and amen to all God has for us.

One

You Were Born for This

We've all been touched and deeply changed by adversity. Your season of adversity could have included a broken relationship. It could have been a time of battling anxiety, illness, loss of someone you loved, financial hardships, or even a pattern of thoughts that tore you down. Every woman's battle is unique.

What I know to be true is that our hearts have been fashioned to face and fight even the hardest of situations. We aren't alone. We have God on our side.

God has great plans for every woman, **but women of our generation are held down and held back not only by adversity but also by crippling self-doubt. Beaten down by an inner monologue that says they'll never be enough, they become drawn to the message of self-empowerment.** This popular, yet unbiblical, mantra preaches that your success and significance depend exclusively on your own hustle. But this message is missing one crucial part of the equation—Jesus.

Without Jesus, success is empty; it's based on our own striving, and it leaves women feeling like they are lacking, have failed, or just aren't enough to achieve their hopes and dreams. We are left feeling like failures because the whole notion that we are solely responsible for our own success or failure places the burden of success and impact and purpose on us alone, apart from Jesus through the power of the Holy Spirit.

We live in a culture that constantly tells us who we should

be as women. We get messages about what we should do, what we are supposed to say, how we should behave, what's good and what's not, how we should look, how we should live, and what we should enjoy.

Society and social media keep selling us an image of a world that doesn't even exist. We're told to eat according to the latest diet trend, work out like it's our job, and hustle our way to happiness. And we're supposed to do these all while looking perfectly made up and put together and with a closet so organized that we personally keep the label-maker business profitable.

It's exhausting.

Here's the thing: we want to do the right things, we want our lives to matter, we want to take care of ourselves, we want to move past the pain and the pandemics, we want to win the fight against adversity, and we want to find some happiness this side of heaven. But there are so many mixed messages and so much confusion combined with our own self-doubt that we get stuck, throw up our hands, and wonder exactly where our place is.

A Woman's Place

Have you heard someone say, even jokingly, that "a woman's place is in the kitchen" or board room or fill-in-the-blank? (I have often thought a woman's place is at Target. Can I get an amen?) For Christians, however, a woman belongs in only one place: squarely in the center of wherever God has sent her.

A woman's place is changing the world around her.

A woman's place isn't doing things just for selfish ambition but because God has given her gifts the world needs.

A woman's place is walking in the strength that comes from God.

A woman's place is with her Savior, led by the Holy Spirit

wherever God calls her—taking action, rejecting lies, stepping up, dreaming big, being brave, learning how to fight and then to fly.

To live a life of meaning, we must know the source of all good things, God Almighty. For us to be fully alive as women, we need to be tapped into our creator, receiving power and wisdom and direction from God.

This is why the message today's generation of women are receiving makes me so angry. God is calling his daughters to more. He does not call us to be the heroes of our own stories. *He* is the hero of our story. God is calling women to partner with him, to be a force in a barren, broken world, woven with weariness.

These two messages—"You go. You've got this and you're going to be amazing," and "You go. Jesus has got this, and with him you're going to be amazing!"—may look similar because they both empower women to rise up and step out and accomplish great things in the world. But the message of God and the popular message of this world couldn't be more different.

> GOD IS CALLING WOMEN TO PARTNER WITH HIM, TO BE A FORCE IN A BARREN, BROKEN WORLD, WOVEN WITH WEARINESS.

One is based solely on an individual's capacity. The other is exponentially more powerful and lasting because it brings together a woman and the power of God in her life, a power that will lead and guide and multiply her efforts, resulting in something eternally significant.

Now is the time to reject the former and embrace the latter, to take action, reject lies, step up, dream big, be brave, learn how to fight, and stand strong because the power of the Holy Spirit is in us.

The Holy Spirit tells us it's time to stop playing small and to embrace the great gifts God has given us. When women—created by God on purpose—play small, the entire world misses out, our gifts atrophy, and we feel the lack in our lives.

The Groundswell Moment

The good news is that the ground beneath us is shifting, thank God, as women are rising up and refusing to crumble under the weight of the adversities and arbitrary limitations placed on them. Many are waking up to the knowledge that they were created with powerful callings.

We are women of God, standing strong together, no longer willing to accept what others say about us, no longer content to live under limits that have been set for us. We are rejecting the stories we have believed about our lives and are replacing them with God's scripts for us. We are waking up and deciding that self-doubt has held us back from what God has for us long enough.

This groundswell moment is not only important but also inspired. God is doing something in the hearts of women, and I recognize this yearning because I've felt it myself. When God called me to take what seemed like an impossible risk for him, I balked, self-doubt snuck in, and I told him life was good enough already. I didn't want to obey; I didn't want to step out of the boat; I was happy enough, comfortable enough, satisfied enough.

This state of enoughness didn't scare me. Rather, it seemed like an improvement over the situation that held back many of my female forerunners and friends.

For generations, we as women were convinced we weren't enough. Continually living and feeling like we somehow weren't enough was crushing and prevented us from becoming who we were created to be. So we cried out, "I am enough!" We bought T-shirts, got tattoos, put "I am enough" on our letter boards, and lived the "enough" life to the fullest.

The "enough" movement has encouraged women to speak up when we've historically been silenced. We have fought for positions and pay, for the right to be valued for more than what we wear, how we look, how we educate our children, or whether or not we work outside the home. We value ourselves and our feelings in ways that wouldn't have happened fifty or even thirty years ago.

All this time we thought shouting "I am enough!" would rally women to celebrate their gifts, but is it simply a way to settle for less? "Enough" was meant to be the first step in women embracing their gifts, but far too many stop there.

Many women feel that enough isn't good enough anymore. In recent years I awakened to God wanting more than just *enough* for my life. Many women I respect who are also sensitive to God's voice tell me that they too have had enough of enough. The wrestling we feel within us—that there is more, that we are more—is intended to move us toward what God has for us.

In today's modern world, the phrase "playing small" is something you hear related to how women interact with the world around them. Playing small is a defense mechanism that says, "If I stay over here and make myself invisible, if I stay in the shadows, no one will notice me. They won't notice my flaws, my insecurities, or my differences. And if they don't notice me, they can't confirm my inner monologue of self-doubt." When I was growing up, before I knew how to play small, I heard the messages of others that told me I was weird, different, unworthy of friendship or love. I took those messages in, owning them as truth, and learned to play small. Now that I'm an adult, those beliefs have set me up: self-doubt tries to take me out and aims to steal the future God planned for me.

Because you're reading this book, I'm guessing you're ready to

> WE'VE SETTLED FOR LESS INSTEAD OF CELEBRATING OUR DREAMS AND GIFTS.

shake off "enough," defeat self-doubt, and move into God's purpose for your life. You feel that God has more for you.

Do any of the following scenarios sound familiar?

Do your friends, pastors, siblings, or parents often remind you that you're capable of more than you can imagine?

Have you begun to have new dreams—starting a business, adopting a child, starting a community garden, writing a book, launching a new initiative—that seem impossible unless God performs a mighty miracle?

Do you feel dissatisfied by the status quo and sense a restlessness that you can't quite put your finger on? Are you often overcome by a feeling that God may be calling you into something life altering?

If so, maybe you've had enough of enough too. Maybe you're done with self-doubt keeping you locked up in a prison. Perhaps it's time for you to find the extraordinary calling God has planted in you.

God isn't calling us to live an *enough* life. He's calling each of us to live an *abundant* life, which is to say, a *more-than-enough* life. He's calling us to walk in our gifts, to overcome our self-doubt, to start living out our purposes, and to stand strong.

The Enemy's Plan for Your Life

Since the fall of humankind, the enemy has been focused on keeping women silent, making women believe they are insignificant, and convincing them they are second class and powerless. He whispers in our ears and our hearts that we don't have what it takes: we've made too many mistakes; we're too uneducated; our pants are a few sizes too big; we're too old, too young, or too plain. But God . . .

The enemy wants you to believe you are insignificant. But God says he knows the very number of hairs on your head (Matthew 10:30).

The enemy wants you to believe the lie that what has been your past, and what is your present, will always be your future. But God calls you chosen, called out of darkness into marvelous light (1 Peter 2:9).

The enemy wants you to focus on all the reasons you can't instead of focusing on the God who can.

This is a common tactic of the enemy because it works. When we agree with the lies of the enemy instead of agreeing with what God says about us, we stay stuck, insecure, and focused on ourselves. Self-doubt is one of the most powerful tools in the enemy's toolbox. When we feel we've had enough of enough, and we're ready for more, ready to step out in faith, the enemy fires a few effective blows that can take us out.

The enemy of your soul whispers that you are prideful to want more, that you don't have what it takes. He lies and says you would already have realized your dream if God wanted it for you. He whispers that your place is to be quiet and stop dreaming of stepping out in faith; he lies and says that your future will look like your past; he sneers that your mistakes are a millstone you will never leave behind.

> DON'T FOCUS ON THE REASONS YOU CAN'T. FOCUS ON THE GOD WHO CAN.

Sometimes it's easier to believe the enemy's lies over the leading God plants in our hearts. It's easier to believe our self-doubt than it is to stand strong in the knowledge that God will give us everything we need in order to do what he calls us to do.

The prison of self-doubt has locked up women for too long. It's time to believe God and shake off the chains. We must decide to live like we believe that what God says is true.

When we take God seriously, we learn to take ourselves seriously. When we take ourselves seriously, like God wants us to, we can step into our gifts and callings. When we step into our gifts and callings, we can change the world.

Calling You to More than Enough

We all share one purpose—to know Jesus and tell others about him. That's it. That's our purpose. But our callings? Our callings are wild and wonderful and ever-changing, depending on the season of life we're in.

I've coached thousands of women in business and ministry over the last twelve years. Many of these women, when I meet one-on-one with them, share with me that they have experienced a moment of stirring to more. They will usually glance around the room and then whisper something like, "Alli, I just can't help but feel like God is calling me to do something great in this world." And every time a woman makes this confession, it's like she is sharing some giant secret worthy of shame. There should be no shame when we sense a call to do great things. Every one of those feelings is a gift from God.

> GOD WILL GIVE YOU EVERYTHING YOU NEED IN ORDER TO DO WHAT HE CALLS YOU TO DO.

I could just about bet that whether you are a stay-at-home mom, a woman in college excited about starting a career, an entrepreneur hustling to get everything done, a nurse caring for someone with cancer or the coronavirus, or a CEO of a large company, *you* have that same whispering deep down. In its own unique way, it whispers, "You are made to do great things in this world. You are made for more."

Have you felt it?

Are you familiar with this little tug at your soul?

Do you keep waiting for someone to give you permission to go for it, even though God already has by placing the desire in your heart?

Or have you been ignoring it for so long that you almost forgot it was there?

That feeling inside you is God calling you to a new adventure, to growth, to a higher level of understanding, to a better future.

So what does a call to accomplish great things in the world look like? It may look like caring for your family with strength and patience in the middle of a pandemic, being the first one in your family to graduate from college, penning the next great American novel, volunteering at church to remind hurting hearts that God loves them, or launching a business that will shake up an industry. In whatever way it manifests for you, the feeling that you are meant for more exists for a reason.

You may not feel like you can do what he has placed in your heart, but guess what? The greatness God is calling you to has nothing to do with how you feel. It has nothing to do with your weakness, your failures, your hang-ups, or your bad habits. It has everything to do with God working in and through you so that you can stand strong.

But what does standing strong mean? It is not about striving, personal achievement, or building ourselves up. It's all about yielding

STANDING STRONG MEANS GETTING OUT OF YOUR OWN WAY AND LETTING GOD WORK IN AND THROUGH YOU.

to God and getting out of our own way. Standing strong is about growing strong. It's about getting unstuck, tapping into the power God gives us, utilizing and developing our gifts, and living the more-than-enough life he offers.

Standing strong is about acknowledging God's strength in us as well as our own strength in choosing to stand strong in his power. He has called us to a beautiful partnership, not because he needs us but because he wants to share the meaningful work and the goodness of his kingdom. We are joint heirs in the here and now, called to more in the here and now, and I don't know about you, but that truth inspires me to stand up and stand strong in God's power, no matter what life throws my way.

When I first sat down to write this book, I prayed over what God wanted me to share with you. Each time I prayed about the heart of this work, I heard my mom's prayer for me as a young girl: that I would become a great woman of God, strong in my faith and fearless as I faced the future.

As a girl I never appreciated that prayer, but the small phrase "great woman of God" has stuck with me. God has used it many times to remind me of my mother's prayer and his calling on my life.

I believe that God wants to help you live out that prayer too.

Defining a Great Woman of God

A great woman of God rejects the world's feel-good, fake-empowerment, cheerleading messages.

A great woman of God is full of faith in the One who makes her great.

A great woman of God knows that her power is not derived from her own strength but from God's.

A great woman of God knows that her value is not derived
from what she does but from what God does in and
through her.
A great woman of God discovers that what her courage sets
in motion can benefit others for generations to come.

Every woman, and her calling in each season of life, is special and unique. Some seasons have us fighting in the middle of
the battle—planning, leading, and seeing lives changed because
of our work. Those seasons feel so purposeful because measuring
our impact is easy. But sometimes God calls us to seasons of rest,
when it may feel like we are sitting on the sidelines watching life
go by. Those seasons are purposeful too because they are seasons of
preparation. God is just as much at work in us when he calls us to
rest as he is when he calls us to engage.

Uncovering the life God has for you is an exciting adventure
that looks different in different seasons.

We have many great women of God to whom we can look.

Sarah realized her greatness when God followed through on
his ridiculous promise (Genesis 21).
Jochebed found her greatness when she used her wisdom to
save her son (Exodus 2).
Deborah used her greatness to step up when no one else
would (Judges 4).
Abigail learned what it meant to be great when she rolled up
her sleeves and saved her household (1 Samuel 25).
Rahab taught us that greatness can look like protecting those
who can't protect themselves (Joshua 2).
Esther showed us that greatness means being willing to take
the ultimate risk, even if you're not sure of the outcome
(Esther 5–7).

The Proverbs 31 woman demonstrated greatness in how she
managed her home and her business (Proverbs 31).

Mary said yes and amen to God in the middle of a possible
risk (Luke 2).

God has a habit of raising up great women in every era, and he
wants you to join this lineage.

If any of these great women of God in the Bible were sitting in
front of us, I bet they would say they didn't feel they were great at
the time. They would laugh and shake their heads. They would tell
us stories of their ordinary lives and how they trusted and obeyed
God in seemingly mundane ways. In other words, they were just
like us.

You were born for this—to shake off the limitations that others
have imposed on your life. You were born to overcome the adversity
that you fear will overtake you. You were born to tear down the false
beliefs you have about yourself and to embrace the calling God is
wooing you toward.

Are you ready to let go of the self-doubt that's holding you back?

Are you ready to let God strengthen you in the face of adversity?

Are you ready to stand strong, great woman of God?

Then you must begin by learning to declare three simple words:
yes and amen.

I Want You to Remember

*At the end of each chapter, I'm including a few key takeaways to
remember, discussion questions to answer, and action points to help
you fully discover the great woman of God you were created to be.
Grab a journal and maybe a small group of friends, and let's dive in
together.*

God isn't calling us to live an *enough* life. He's calling each of us to live an *abundant* life.

Don't focus on the reasons you can't. Focus on the God who can.

God will give you everything you need to do what he calls you to do.

Standing strong means getting out of your own way and letting God work in and through you.

Discussion Questions

1. A woman's place is anywhere God sends her. Where do you feel "sent to" in your current season?
2. What holds you back from wholeheartedly believing you are a great woman of God?
3. Do you believe that what God says about you is true? Why or why not?

Action Steps

Prayer: Have you felt a tug in your soul for something more? Consider this: that feeling could be God calling you to a new adventure, calling you to growth, calling you to a new level of understanding, calling you to your future. Today, bring that tug to the Lord in prayer. Ask him to illuminate your one next step into what he has called you to.

Journal: Make a list of the places God has called you to in past seasons (for example, work, home, school). Then list the blessings from each of those past places that you still carry with you in your current season (for example, lessons learned, skills developed, relationships gained). Even though your many seasons and places may be diverse, God remains intentional in your journey.

Practice: Instead of focusing on the reasons why you can't, turn your focus to the God who can. Find one Bible promise that resonates with you. Place this verse where you can see it frequently throughout your day (for example, bathroom mirror, car dashboard, phone wallpaper). Every time you see it, say it out loud and then say, "Yes and amen." Take note of how reading, speaking, hearing, and agreeing with truth renews your mind.

Two

Step Out from Hiding

Here I Am, Lord

When I was growing up in the foothills of East Tennessee, something shaped me into a fierce introvert. I enjoyed being alone, plain and simple. While other kids ran in the sunshine or chased fireflies, I walked the aisles of the public library, scooping up as many books as my tiny arms could hold. The librarian, Margie, and I were on a first-name basis, and we often engaged in deep philosophical conversations about books. (Totally normal for an eleven-year-old, right?)

As I grew, I still preferred reading books in my bedroom to attending social events with my friends. Books were safe. They demanded nothing from me. They had no expectations of how I would act or react, and they didn't care about how stylish my outfit was or if my crazy curls were in vogue. My lack of athletic ability and the thickness of my thighs were of no concern. My books offered perpetual welcome and asked nothing in return.

To this day, I feel uncomfortable in crowds. I grow acutely aware of every nerve ending in my body. My hands, so capable of flipping through the pages of a book, seem large and disconnected. I wonder, "What the heck do I do with my hands?

Do I hold them, twist them, allow them to hang at my sides?" Sometimes the voice in my head yells, "Alli, for the love, do something with your hands. Everyone is looking at your hands!" When my hands aren't concerning me, I am filled with dread over what to say. With every lull in the conversation, I never fail to feel like everyone is waiting for me to say something clever, cute, or funny.

My introverted nature probably kept me out of trouble growing up. The last place you were going to find me was at a crowded party full of teenagers with more hormones than sense. But what served me well in high school doesn't serve me well in the career world, so I have had to force myself to step beyond my world of books and into the real world.

I like to call myself a high-functioning introvert. On the one hand, I adore being around people, but on the other hand, being around people drains my battery like a toddler drains a juice box. After all is said and done, I have to find a quiet corner where I can hibernate and recharge.

The beauty of adulthood is that all the weird facts I collected from my well-read childhood serve me well when conversation inevitably lags. I can drive a conversation like nobody's business. And I even know what to do with my hands now. Not only that, I'm an introvert who loves events. Whether it's a group of ten or ten thousand, I want to be there, whether I'm attending, hosting, or speaking. I love it all. Give me a microphone at a corporate event, a church, or a business conference, and I'll have something to say.

That's why a nerdy, bookish girl like me grew into a woman who, for six years, *ran* the Blissdom Conference, one of the largest conferences focused on teaching women how to build a successful business using online tools. I think Margie would be proud.

Stepping Out

My story makes sense only if you know how I moved from being a bedroom bookworm to a high-functioning introvert with an extrovert's career.

I married right out of college and became a stay-at-home mom. At thirty-two, I was loving life, raising my boys, and supporting my husband's career. But four weeks after the birth of our fifth son (yes, that's five sons), our lives were turned upside down, and life as we knew it came crashing down around us. It was right at the beginning of the big recession in 2008, and my husband, Mark, had lost his job the year before. We waited for a new job to open up, praying all the while that God would let us stay in Nashville, but it was not to be. Our savings ran dry, we lost our home, and we filed for bankruptcy.

With our life in shambles, my husband and I began the hard work of piecing it back together. We saved two portable storage units' worth of personal belongings and then moved in with my grandfather. Falling that far was beyond humbling. Some days it was difficult to get out of bed. But every day, Mark and I drove to McDonald's to let the kids play in the PlayPlace while we used the free Wi-Fi. Mark applied for new jobs anywhere (we were too desperate at this point to limit the search to Nashville), and I googled "How to start a business from home." With my old laptop with missing keys, forty-two dollars in business start-up money, and a search engine, I was ready to take on the digital world.

After a long summer of applying for jobs, by August, Mark had a job offer at a hospital outside Nashville. We moved two and a half hours away from my grandfather's house, grateful for his generosity to us in our time of need. Happier than a toddler with a bag of candy, we drove back to the town we loved, thanking God for new beginnings.

I kept learning, focused and determined to build a business from home that could sustain our family should we ever suffer such a financial setback again. Thanks to my childhood love of reading and the power of the internet, I learned that I could build just about anything I dreamed up. I still joke, "With God and Google, we are unstoppable!"

I had been blogging for years, long before our bankruptcy, so with friends I knew both online and in person, I cofounded the Blissdom Conference. Blissdom was a conference for women who were using their gifts online to build businesses.

WITH GOD AND GOOGLE, WE ARE UNSTOPPABLE.

I was an introvert running a conference, which is roughly equivalent to an elephant wearing a bow tie. I knew nothing about running a conference, and I knew little about how to conduct myself in a crowd of people. But as I watched the next season of my life unfold, I was surprised to find that Blissdom not only brought financial security to our family, it also brought me joy.

There was something about running Blissdom that felt like the missing piece of the puzzle in my life. Running the conference took every aspect of my well-read childhood, all the life skills I had acquired as a wife and mom, my expertise from the blogging world, and the tenacity I was developing as an entrepreneur and put it all together to make sense of the longing to help others that God had placed deep inside me.

I was walking in my calling, and everything felt so right. My family was thriving, my work was thriving, and I was fulfilled.

Then, seemingly out of the blue, God nudged my heart that my time with Blissdom was over. I had to explain to my business partners that God had told me I needed to walk away from the business we had built together. When you tell people that "Jesus told me" to take some crazy, wild, illogical step, you hear one of three responses: they say, "That's amazing. Nice job obeying!", or they give you a serious side-eye, or they think you are outright crazy. Luckily, my partners handled my resignation with grace.

So much had changed in our lives since our financial downfall. As my business took off and became a success, Mark had retired from his job to be a stay-at-home dad, focusing on raising our tribe of testosterone. I was the sole source of our family's income, so walking away from Blissdom meant not only giving up a company I loved so much but also giving up our financial security.

But I knew in my heart of hearts that God was calling me away.

Leaving Blissdom broke my heart. I was devastated, and it made no sense whatsoever that God would call me away from something that had finally made me feel whole. But God had brought me from a season of failure to a season of success, so I had faith he would carry us through this as well. I knew he had to have a purpose, but it was lost on me as to what it was.

In faith, I stepped out into an unknown future with God, who offered all the security I could ever hope for.

Are You Kidding Me?

Throughout my years at Blissdom, I met a lot of women who owned their own companies, who led large corporations, and who respected me as a businesswoman. With my source of income gone, I took what I had and what I knew, and I launched a new career—coaching business owners.

Getting anything off the ground is hard work, and I worked so hard that year building another new business. My business was growing and thriving, but don't for one second think it was a year full of rainbows and unicorns. It was a year of wrestling and questioning. I continually questioned God. "Why did you take me out of something where I could help thousands of women to coaching, where I'm helping just one woman at a time?"

Though I obeyed God by surrendering something I loved, I was in a season of loss. My new business was doing well financially, yet most days I felt panicked by some impending doom. The voice of the enemy was a constant distraction that made me feel as though my work in the world no longer mattered.

When I first imagined following God's call to leave Blissdom, I dreamed it would look like a scene from a Disney movie—birds would fly around my head, a magic path would unfold in front of me, and I would burst into song about how everything in my life was great and made sense.

But it didn't happen that way. I obeyed, but I continued to wrestle with what God was doing in my life.

I learned that obedience sometimes feels like a gut-punch.

Then one day everything shifted again. Evangelist Christine Caine of The A21 Campaign asked me to help her build and launch a ministry focused on developing and supporting women—Propel Women. She announced that I was the woman she needed to help her build this dream in her heart, and the rest, as they say, is history.

Propel Women was my dream job.

I pushed pause on my coaching business, and although the Propel office is in California, I ran the operations from my home office in Nashville. I spent my days knocking out projects designed to empower women to be all God had called them to be. Soon I was running events again. And you know how much my introverted self loves gathering women.

It was an honor to work through Propel with women who were heroes of my faith, women I had listened to and learned from for years. It made perfect sense that God had called me away from Blissdom and my coaching business to focus on ministry. Finally, his plan for my life made sense. A career in ministry had been my ultimate goal, and Blissdom was a necessary step toward that end.

I was living the dream, firmly planted and growing in God's will for my life.

Until I went to Austin.

I had been in my role as COO of Propel for three years when I traveled to Austin, Texas, for the IF:Gathering conference, an annual women's event. I was ready for two days of worship and teaching.

Here's the thing about me. When I attend an event, I leave the noise, pressure, and to-do lists of my normal life behind. I'm there to visit with women I love, meet new friends, and grow. I always arrive at events hopeful for what God will do and say.

But I wasn't expecting what he would do and say that day.

As the crowds gathered, I chatted with my friends, completely unaware that my life was about to change forever. One single moment swept in unannounced and radically redefined my new normal.

Maybe you've had those moments too, the ones that change your life in an instant. Perhaps it was seeing the two lines on your pregnancy test or learning your promotion came with a hefty pay raise and a move to a new city. Maybe it was hearing your diagnosis for the first time or having your eyes opened to new truth.

Sometimes a single moment can change your life forever.

For me that moment came during the first worship song that night in Austin. I can't even remember what the song was. But I sensed God saying, "Leave." When God speaks to me, I don't audibly hear it. I just know it. It's typically only a few words, but somehow he gives me clarity on the exact context.

With a racing heart and sweaty palms, I sat in my chair for fear I might faint. I can't tell you exactly how I knew it, but I knew what "leave" meant.

He wasn't asking me to walk out the doors of the event that night. I knew he wasn't telling us to move to a new city. I knew he meant it was time to leave my job.

It felt like a blow out of nowhere.

"Why, Lord?"

Why was he asking me to leave . . . again?

Wasn't ministry what I was called to do?

First I had to leave Blissdom, and now I needed to leave Propel, a ministry I helped build and loved to serve? *WHY WAS I THE GIRL WHO ALWAYS HAD TO LEAVE?*

Was I not doing what God wanted me to? Was I disappointing him in some way?

I had a million unanswered questions for God, but I didn't receive any answers.

All I knew for certain was that I was not where I was supposed to be.

Where Are You?

After the serpent tempted Eve and she and Adam ate the forbidden fruit that brought sin into the world, they, for the first time, hid from God. Of course, he knew where they were, but he asked anyway, "Where are you?" It wasn't a rhetorical question. He expected an answer, not for his benefit but for theirs. They needed to answer.

God's first question for humankind is one he still loves to ask us today.

Where are you?

Where are you in life?

Where are you with your relationships?

Where are you with your dreams?

Where are you?

He asks us this question because sometimes we need a wake-up call.

But sometimes we resist wake-up calls.

I sat slumped in my seat and stared out over the crowd in denial. "Why can't God tell me good things?" I wondered. "Why can't he ask me to do things that are at least not so painful. Ugh. Why, God?"

I gave up my company to work in full time ministry, and now he was calling me out of this too? The room spun and I felt sick.

The buzz of my phone interrupted my self-pity session. It was my friend Bianca, who was backstage preparing to teach the next session.

"Hey. Are you busy?" Bianca asked. "Can you come backstage and pray over me before I teach?"

Bianca and I have been friends for years, but we couldn't be more different. She's from LA and she's stylish, with a natural fiery passion about her. I'm from Nashville, with a style best described as "trying not to look like the mom of five sons," and I delight in my goofiness. We are a wonderfully odd couple. She's a forever friend. You know, my ride or die.

A lot of women I meet have their ride-or-die friends too. The kind of friends we call when we need prayer, need to rant, or need to hide a body. The ones who are on standby with a Bible, a Catwoman suit, and duct tape in the trunk of their car because you never know what enemy you'll be fighting together that day. These are the friends who speak both encouragement and hard truth over us when it's needed.

I set aside the pounding questions in my head and made my way backstage to pray over Bianca. I prayed that God would speak through her to every woman in that gathering and that he would use her in mighty ways for the kingdom. I prayed for chains to break, new revelation to be revealed, and for the women in attendance to walk out of the room wanting more of Jesus than when they entered. Little did I know that I was praying for myself.

After we prayed, we chatted for about five seconds, and I blurted out, "God told me to leave!" I didn't give any context. Before I could say anything else, Bianca hugged me and exclaimed, "I've known he was calling you away. I could just feel it."

We stared at each other in awe, laughed, hugged, and I said, "What in the world am I going to do now?"

Bianca laughed and said, "Alli, God will tell you. And it's going to be good."

We took a selfie together in her dressing room mirror to remember the moment, you know, to mark this very spiritual milestone, and a few minutes later she was teaching the Bible while I was sitting back in the crowd wondering what in the world God was doing.

It was time for another shift. He was calling me out into the unknown again, just as he had done five years before. I could look back and see that when he called me to leave Blissdom, it was to do something great for the kingdom. But I confused doing something great for the kingdom with being in ministry and accomplishing tasks on a large scale.

Sometimes doing something great in this world means doing things no one will ever see or know about.

I sat in that concert hall for the rest of the evening with my mind racing.

I didn't know what was next. But I knew what was no more.

So—where are *you*?

Are you in a season of life that is calm and you know you are where God has called you, doing what he has called you to do? If so, rest in that. Or are you in a season like I was, where God is nudging you to stop doing something, maybe even something you love? If he is, let it go. You could even be in a season of seeing your dreams become a reality, dreams that have been in your heart for years, buried under the weight of life. If that's you, celebrate the freedom and enjoy your dreams.

Or maybe you're like my friend Jennifer, frozen in fear, unable to move forward. God keeps whispering to her to write, but that girl hasn't written a word yet. It's like she's waiting on God to send her a memo that says, "Write a devotional for college-age women," or "Write a book on how to parent girls." She's overwhelmed by the unknown, waiting on who knows who to grant her permission and stuck in thinking that if she feels self-doubt, she shouldn't move forward.

Let me tell you, sister, God does his best work in the mystery. In our weakness, in our lack of ability, in our mess, he does amazing work, using us in such a way that *he* is the only explanation.

Are you where God desires you to be?

Or are you, like Eve, hiding?

Are you ignoring his call to leave, to stay, to strike out into a new frontier?

What would life look like if you stepped out from hiding and answered, "Here I am, Lord, and I'm ready for whatever you have next!"

Where Is God Calling You?

As I sat in that concert hall stunned and afraid, the reality that my life was about to turn upside down sank in, and I felt alone. I realized I had a choice to make. Was I going to believe God was telling me to step out in faith into the unknown, or was I going to ignore him and continue the path I was on?

I had to accept that this season was coming to an end. I was standing on the edge of an unknown future, and I had to find the courage to take the next step.

God takes it seriously when we let our lack of faith hold us back from taking the next step on our faith journey. Did you know that? In the parable of the talents (Matthew 25:14–30), Jesus is clear that, as his followers, we are called to take action in faith with the gifts and talents he has given us.

Jesus tells a parable about a master who went on a journey and left three servants behind to manage his "talents." The talent was an ancient unit of currency. To help you gain perspective, a single talent was worth more than any of these servants would have made in his lifetime. Each servant received a number of talents on the basis of that servant's *known* ability level. This was a wise master. He knew what his servants were capable of. One servant received five talents, one received two, and one received one.

When the master returned, he discovered the trusted servants had handled their talents with different outcomes. The man to whom he gave five talents had doubled them, presenting his master with ten talents upon his return. The master replied, "Well done, good and faithful servant! You were faithful over a few things; I will put you in charge of many things. Share your master's joy" (Matthew 25:21 CSB).

The servant who was given two talents doubled his as well and was praised just the same.

But the servant with one talent had a different story.

The man who had received one talent also approached and said, "Master, I know you. You're a harsh man, reaping where you haven't sown and gathering where you haven't scattered seed. [This guy clearly did not know how to butter up his boss.] So I was afraid and went off and hid your talent in the ground. See, you have what is yours."

His master replied to him, "You evil, lazy servant! If you knew that I reap where I haven't sown and gather where I haven't scattered, then you should have deposited my money with the bankers, and I would have received my money back with interest when I returned.

"So take the talent from him and give it to the one who has ten talents. For to everyone who has, more will be given, and he will have more than enough. But from the one who does not have, even what he has will be taken away from him. And throw this good-for-nothing servant into the outer darkness, where there will be weeping and gnashing of teeth" (Matthew 25:24–30 CSB).

I can't help but compare this parable to our everyday lives.

Have you ever felt pain, felt stuck, or felt regret because you didn't have the faith to step out and take action? Our problem, much like that of the lazy servant, isn't in our abilities or our callings; it's in our perception of the One who called us in the first place.

Fear and a lack of faith in him sometimes stop me and can threaten to stop you.

Every time we behave like that unfaithful servant and bury our gifts instead of taking action and using them, we say with our behavior, "I don't trust you. I don't trust that you are a good God. I don't trust that you know what's best or that you will be there to help me accomplish what you planted in my heart."

The One who called you, the One who placed your dream in your heart, is the same God who created the world and is holding it all together today. **And he takes your talent seriously. He doesn't want you to bury your talent; he wants you to use it for his glory.**

> **THE GOD WHO CALLED YOU IS THE SAME GOD WHO CREATED THE WORLD.**

God, the creator of heaven and earth is calling you—yes *you*—to do great things.

He is calling you to participate in endings and beginnings, to build and to nurture.

God is calling you to partner with him to accomplish great plans that might not make sense right now, just like that night in Austin when it seemed like God was calling me away from the only "great thing" I'd ever done.

GOD IS FAITHFUL TO FINISH WHAT HE STARTS IN YOU.

What God has for you may not make sense right now, but that is where faith comes in. God is faithful to finish what he starts in you. But believing that and taking action are 100 percent up to you. He doesn't give us a step-by-step guide with a clear description of where we are going. He lights up just enough of the road ahead of us for us to see and take one step at a time.

He's calling you to step out from hiding and say, "Here I am, Lord."

I Want You to Remember

Sometimes doing something great in this world means doing things no one will ever see or know.

The One who called you, the One who placed your dream in your heart, is the same God who created the world and is holding it all together today. And he takes your talent very seriously. He doesn't want you to bury your talent; he wants you to use it for his glory.

God, the creator of heaven and earth is calling you to do great things. He is calling you to end things, begin things, build things, grow things, nurture things.

God is faithful to finish what he starts in you.

Discussion Questions

1. God asked Adam and Eve, "Where are you?" Are you currently where God wants you to be? Is he calling you to stay or leave? Start or stop? Hold on or let go?
2. Consider the parable of the talents. Are you stewarding your money, gifts, talents, time, and so forth by using them, or are you hiding them?
3. God is calling you to partner with him to do great things. What do you believe God wants to accomplish with you during this season?

Action Steps

Prayer: Often we hide because we don't know what to do. James 1:5 tells us that when we lack wisdom, we can ask God for it, and he will give us a generous amount of it. Bring any lack of clarity about your calling to the Lord in prayer. Ask him specifically for wisdom. Record what you sense he is telling you.

Journal: No matter what God calls you to do, the first step of obedience is to respond, "Here I am, Lord." List the worries, doubts, or fears that are keeping you from stepping out. Then cross out each item and write, "Here I am, Lord" as a demonstration of your obedience.

Practice: Find a friend to partner with you in prayer about what you believe God is asking you to do. Ask specifically for prayer, not advice. Practice hearing from God for yourself, and ask your prayer partner to pray for a clear connection between you and God.

Three

Remember Who You Are

I Am a Daughter of the King

The 1990s remains one of the most iconic decades in pop culture. It has been called the "golden age of sitcoms," with hits from *Friends* to *Seinfeld*, from *The Fresh Prince of Bel-Air* to *Full House*. It gave us boy bands like NSYNC and the Backstreet Boys and girl bands like the Spice Girls and Destiny's Child. Thank you, 1990s. We didn't deserve you and can never repay you for the gift that is Justin Timberlake.

But of all the life-altering inventions of that decade, nothing, and I mean nothing, holds a candle to its films. What would Christmas be without Kevin McCallister being left home alone? Can you remember the first time you saw *Titanic*? I am still convinced there was room for Jack on that door Rose was floating on. And don't get me started on the brilliance of *The Shawshank Redemption* and *Braveheart*.

When a friend of mine recently asked which nineties movie was my all-time favorite, I didn't blink. "*The Lion King*, of course," I said as if there were only one right answer. If there was any place you'd find my childhood self—other than the library—it was the movie theater. So you can imagine how my heart skipped a beat when I first heard Disney was developing

The Lion King as part of its effort to remake its animated classics into live-action features.

If you haven't seen this film in a while, let me jog your memory. A young lion named Simba blames himself for the untimely death of his father, King Mufasa. In a fit of shame and sorrow, Simba flees to the wilderness where he grows up, not in the strength of his purpose and calling but instead hanging out with a meerkat and a warthog with a flatulence problem (every mother of sons can relate). In the wilderness, Simba traded his calling as a king for endless days of goofing around while hidden away in anonymity.

The plot shifts when Simba's long-lost mandrill friend, Rafiki, discovers his whereabouts and helps the young lion understand who he is and who he is meant to be. Rafiki brings him to a field where the spirit of King Mufasa appears in the sky and says, "You have forgotten me, and because you have forgotten me, you have forgotten who you are. Simba, remember who you are."

Although I've seen this movie many times over the years, when I saw it in theaters for the first time as an adult, its message spoke to me in a new way. "Remember who you are." It's about the best advice I can think of for the countless women today who also have been hiding out in the wilderness, running from their callings.

Great woman of God, you are a daughter of the king. And our God is not just some king of the jungle; he's the ruler of the universe. Have you, like Simba, forgotten who you are? Have you forgotten who God is? Have you forgotten that he watches over you, protects you, empowers you, and lives in you?

Maybe you were never taught this truth and are discovering it for the first time. Or perhaps you know this in your heart, but you've long since buried it and left it behind. Either way, it is time to remember who you are.

Forgotten Identities

When we forget who we are in God, we are at risk of believing the world's lies:

> Your body is the most important thing about you.
> What you do and what you achieve define you.
> You'll never overcome your past.
> You have to prove your worth.
> You are responsible for everyone's happiness.

Each of these lies is custom designed to distract us, discourage us, and depress us. Small and insignificant on their own, these lies compound over time until they feel true. As the constant day-to-day reminder of these lies wears us down, we begin to doubt who we are.

Lies Attack Our Identity

Simba, living in self-imposed exile in the wilderness, lost his identity. When he had no memory of who he was and no memory of who his father was, he had no hope, no vision, and no strength.

How is that different from us?

We live in our own wilderness, with no real vision for who we are, because we forget the nature of God—how he loves us, makes us new, gives us a purpose, and calls us his daughters.

The truth is, we are in the direct lineage of the king of the universe. That is our true identity, and no lie of the enemy has the power to steal that from us.

Identity Is Essential to God

Today we name children using any number of methods: maybe it's a family name, perhaps it's from pop culture, or maybe we just like the sound of it. But in ancient times, a name carried significant meaning. It represented who a person was and who they would become; it represented identity.

Sarai became Sarah. As Sarai, her name meant princess, the daughter of a king. But when God changed her name to Sarah, he changed her identity as well: no longer "princess" but forever known as the "mother of nations."

Saul became Paul. Saul was a brutal murderer of Christians of the early church and was radically saved on the road to Damascus. But as Paul, he was a disciple of Christ and wrote many of the books of the New Testament.

Simon became Peter. Simon was a fisherman. But when the Lord called him to be one of the first disciples, he named him Peter, the "rock" on which he would build his church (Matthew 16:18). And as Peter, he became the leader of the early Christian church.

Jacob became Israel. As Jacob, he stole his brother's birthright, married a woman he didn't love, then seven years later married her sister. But as Israel, the Lord used him to establish the twelve tribes of the Jewish nation.

God Cares about Your Identity

God's chosen name, "I am," is a statement of identity. It's evidence that names represent identity and that identity matters.

I hear many women today call themselves and other women in their community daughters of God, but they don't usually explain what that means. But the Bible tells us precisely what it means—we're valuable, we're chosen, we're forgiven, and we're strong.

We're valuable (1 Corinthians 7:23). You were bought at a price. Jesus gave his life for you. There's nothing you can do today to be more or less valuable. You are valuable just as you are. That means your boss doesn't get to define your worth on his worst day. It means you aren't a bad mom when your kid messes up. And your own mistakes don't diminish your value either.

We're chosen (1 Peter 2:9). If you feel disregarded by the world, your spouse, your family, or even your friends, cling to the knowledge that almighty God has hand-selected you. If the person you believed to be your soul mate has walked out the door, know that God selected you as his prize. If you scroll through social media and see your friends hanging out without you, know that God's highlight reel always includes you. You have been chosen.

We're forgiven (1 John 1:9). You don't have to live in shame, because your failures don't define you. From the moment of salvation and throughout the rest of your life, as you confess your sins to God, he forgives you completely, wholly, holding nothing back. The slate is wiped clean.

We're strong (Philippians 4:12–13). God has made you strong, with the ability to survive anything that comes your way. Even when you feel weak and overwhelmed, you're stronger than you think. There is a strength within you that surpasses human understanding.

The Crown of Creation

I've often heard women referred to as the "crown of creation." My only frame of reference for anyone being crowned (other than Disney princesses) is Queen Elizabeth II. I always thought it interesting that she had all the responsibilities of the ruling monarch of England, but she wasn't officially crowned until nearly sixteen months after she ascended the throne. It's as if the whole of it all wasn't quite enough until that moment. The Monarchy was in some way not complete without that crown.

If we think about how and why God created humankind, the same could be said. Creation was somehow not complete without the crown.

We Are Created to Create

"God blessed them, and God said to them, 'Be fruitful, multiply, fill the earth, and subdue it. Rule the fish of the sea, the birds of the sky, and every creature that crawls on the earth'" (Genesis 1:28 CSB). One of the first "jobs" God gave us was to create. We create people. It's no small feat. We grow actual human beings inside our bodies!

And in case that isn't impressive enough, we create art, grow gardens, compose music, build businesses, cook delicious meals, and write books. The list is endless.

God created us to create.

We Are Created to Complement

"Then the LORD God said, "It is not good for the man to be alone. I will make a helper corresponding to him" (Genesis 2:18 CSB). And so the woman, Eve, was created from the rib of Adam because God saw that creation wasn't complete. Eve was created as a "helper corresponding to him." In Hebrew, this word is *ezer kenegdo*. *Ezer* means helper. *Kenegdo* means opposition or against— not opposition like disharmony but balance and support.[1]

Think of two things complementing, balancing, and opposing each other. Imagine a beam or a plank. If you stand it up alone, it will fall over, but if you add another plank and lean them against each other, they support each other. The second plank opposes the weight of the first, and they hold each other up. They are equal but opposite.

God created men and women to live as partners, loving and serving each other.

Ezer is used twenty-one times in the Bible. It is used five times to describe women and sixteen times to describe God as Israel's "helper." I want you to fully grasp this. When *ezer* is used to portray God, the term is one of military defense and protection. When David says his help comes from the Lord, the word for "help" is *ezer*

(Psalm 121). *Ezer* is also used when God is identified as Israel's help and shield (Psalm 115:9). We aren't talking about a "helper" in the sense of picking up someone else's socks or serving your boss coffee. We are talking about someone ready and able to enter battle.

A helper is strong and capable, perfectly suited for whatever and to whomever God calls us.

We are created to complement.

We Are Created to Complete

God made all of creation—every component of the cosmos, every plant, every flower, every animal in the air and in the sea and on the ground. And he made human- kind. And after all that, he stepped back and said, "Hmmm, something's not quite right here." (This is the ALT—Alli Living Translation—of course.)

And he created woman, the literal com- pletion of creation. We can't forget this.

> **DON'T FORGET WHO YOU ARE.**
>
> **DON'T FORGET WHOSE YOU ARE.**

Women were not an afterthought to God. We are the crowning glory. He created us last not because we are less-than but because we are the finishing touch.

I don't think most women have been taught this. Sister, we completed creation!

We are created to be strong and great in this world.

We are great women of God.

That is our identity.

That is *your* identity.

Maybe you have forgotten who you are because you've forgot- ten *whose* you are.

When we focus on the nature of God, his goodness, and the grace and love he extends to us, it is easier to know that our identity is rooted in his strength and not dependent on what we do.

Clothed in Strength

Who comes to mind when you think of a strong woman?

A CEO running her company?
A woman in the Armed Forces?
A woman running for public office because she wants to be the voice of change?

Yes, those are strong women, but they don't represent a complete picture. I also think of a mother rocking her baby; she's not on the cover of *Fast Company*, but she is the picture of strength. What about a young woman working two jobs to pay her way through college? She may not get a gold watch or a celebration party, but who can deny her strength?

What about a woman who is standing strong, getting healthy, and breaking unhealthy patterns in her family that have been there for generations? Her work may be slow, purposeful, and internal, but it will pay dividends for generations to come. How about a wife on her knees praying for restoration in her marriage? She's working as hard as any CEO trying to keep a company afloat.

Think of a woman brave enough to do the work of growth. No one is stronger than the person who faces her weaknesses head-on, willing to change and grow as the Holy Spirit guides. And let's not forget a woman who devotes herself to helping younger women grow. She bears the responsibility of challenging, nurturing, and discipling younger women as commanded in Titus 2.

I have realized over the past twelve years of coaching women in their spiritual walks, their lives, and their businesses that we rarely think of ourselves as strong women. We tend to see ourselves through the lens of our weaknesses, our struggles, and our limitations.

God doesn't want us to view ourselves that way. When he created us, he created us to be strong, the complement to the whole of creation. He clothed us in strength and dignity so that we, with great faith in him, would live life without fear of the future.

In every season of our lives, we are stronger and more courageous than we think, even when we don't recognize it.

In adolescence—when we are entirely unsure of who we are, when the mean girls are the meanest, and when our future seems far too distant to matter—it takes strength to keep showing up in the face of so much uncertainty.

In our twenties, strength is navigating the pressures of college, graduation, finding the right job, establishing community, and dating. It takes courage to deal with constant rejection in a swipe-right world.

In our thirties, we are dauntless and brave, doing our best to ignore the ticking of our biological clocks or, if we have kids, trying to survive the burden of mom guilt. Strength is adulting with balance in a 24/7 world.

In our forties, we are in the prime of our working years, full of productivity and earning potential from years of building our expertise and work history. We begin caring for aging parents who need us, all while watching our role with our kids change as they grow up and begin to leave the nest.

In our fifties and beyond, we enjoy the fruit from the gardens we have planted our whole lives. We coach our grown children, navigate new relationship dynamics, revel in life as a grandparent, and deal with our own aging bodies. Strength is facing loss and major life transitions with grit and grace.

So often we merely hope to survive the day. We don't step back from our lives to gain perspective and marvel at how we are absolutely killing it. Between the sheer amount of information coming at us, all the responsibilities we balance, the way we manage to take care of everybody, the way we walk through hard seasons and remain the rock that everyone needs us to be—we don't stop for even a minute to appreciate just how strong we are.

But you know what? Someone you know thinks you're strong. Let me explain.

Think of a strong woman in your life, that woman you look up to. Someone is looking at you that same way. You are that strong woman to others. *To someone else, you embody what a great woman of God is.*

Maybe it's a woman in your small group.

Maybe it's the kids you teach.

Maybe it's your daughter.

Maybe it's your son.

Maybe it's your neighbor.

Maybe it's your coworker.

Maybe you no longer realize how strong you are. Life got hard, tragedy showed up without warning, and you forgot your strength. Or worse yet, maybe you forgot the *source* of your strength.

Just Say No to Hustle and Try Harder

The good news is, the source of your strength is still there. He has always been there, and he will always be there. But to find your way back takes heart change, a real revelation of who you are and whose you are, not behavioral modification.

Behavioral modification says, "If I work harder, I can fix myself."

Heart change says, "If I partner with God, I can work with him as he takes me where he wants me to go and gives me the strength I need to make these changes."

Women of God can't buy into the false gospel of hustle and try harder. We preach with our lives, and our words share the gospel of life, power, surrender, and grace.

The false gospel of hustle will eventually leave everyone who puts their trust in it feeling like a failure, but the gospel of Jesus is a continual source of strength, purpose, and courage.

Our purpose is to know him. Our mission is to show him.

We have to remember that our callings will look different during each season of life.

This is what tripped me up as I struggled to understand why I had to walk away from both my conference and then the ministry.

When it came to leaving Blissdom, I never understood why God called me to walk away from the company I loved so much. Then when Christine asked me to come and help build the ministry, I told myself that the ministry must be more important than what I was doing in the business world. I assumed that consulting in corporate America and building Blissdom were just phases that helped me move toward working in full-time ministry—you know, the *real* work, my *real* calling.

I saw my work in a ministry as worthy and looked back on my days in a for-profit business as less worthy. I told myself that nothing I could ever do would be as impactful because of the vast numbers of women we were reaching as a ministry.

Then when God so clearly told me to leave my job, I was at a loss. My worth as a woman, as a Christian woman, as a wannabe great woman of God, was so tightly wrapped up in my new ministry that it caused me to believe I must have done something wrong. Had God now found me unworthy to help run such a significant ministry?

In the months after he told me to leave, each time I prayed and begged for more direction and answers, all he whispered back to my soul was the phrase my mom prayed over me years ago: "Great woman of God." *What is that even supposed to mean?* I wondered.

Again I was at a complete loss. Why, when I was working so hard doing something great for a ministry, was I getting called away from it?

What God wanted me to learn was that greatness is in obeying, loving, and trusting him and in living my life well. Being a great woman of God isn't rooted in the kind of success that animates Wall Street, Silicon Valley, and South Beach. It's grounded in God's greatness and what that greatness means for my future.

I had to let go of the lie that my identity was wrapped up in my work.

Perhaps you've also looked for your identity in what you do. You've viewed "purpose" as some combination of profession, perfection, and passion. Find the right job, be the perfect employee, entrepreneur, wife, mother, sister, friend, or daughter and fight for the right causes, then *boom*, your identity will be fulfilled and your purpose will be clear. But becoming a great woman of God is about allowing him to strengthen you *as you walk* into the next season of your life.

As I wrestled with my questions and doubts as to why God was calling me away, I was in California with my coworkers, and we all went to see a movie on opening night. It was the perfect movie for a women's leadership and empowerment ministry to see together— *Wonder Woman*, of course.

As a mom of boys, I love superhero movies. And I've loved Wonder Woman ever since I was a little girl fighting imaginary hooligans in my Wonder Woman Underoos. I even have a costume that I bust out whenever I'm invited to a Halloween party. I go all in as the gold-bracelet-wearing Amazonian powerhouse superhero.

Right in the middle of the movie, there is a scene where the heroine, Diana, finds herself in a battle trench bordering no-man's-land. Here's a quick history lesson: during WWI, the French and the Germans would build trenches and wait for months as they tried to gain a few inches at a time. The area between the two trenches was known as no-man's-land because no man could make it across alive.

After hearing the suffering of the nearby people, Diana learns that the only way to rescue them is to charge enemy lines, cross no-man's-land, clear out the Germans' trench, and make a route to the town where they are holding the villagers.

Her compassion for the innocent victims compels her to act. Throwing off her coat and stepping into her identity as a hero, she climbs out of the bunker and runs toward the enemy with steely determination. (Imagine this next part in glorious slow motion.) Diana draws enemy fire, and as the shots come at her, she deflects them effortlessly with her fabulous golden bracelets and charges ahead. (Are you picturing yourself fighting off bullets with those golden bracelets, or is that just me?)

Reaching the middle of no-man's-land, she lowers herself, places her shield in front of her body, and takes all the fire the enemy can throw at her. As the enemy fires away, she provides cover for the men to attack the trench, and she frees the people in the nearby town.

Diana is the *ezer*, the warrior, in this movie much the same way that you and I, along with women throughout history, are the mighty, capable helpers and warriors in our own stories.

What caught me off guard was that I cried through that whole scene of Diana charging the enemy and taking their fire.

I cried because this is what we do as women.

This is us.

We may not have fabulous golden bracelets that deflect bullets and take on machine guns, but we are women who, when filled with purpose, will charge hell and enemy lines. We are women who create, complement, and complete—women placed on this earth as the solution to problems.

We are wonder women, taking bullets every day, and we don't even realize it.

We sacrifice when the family budget doesn't have enough to go around. We lose sleep when we have more to do than time to do it. Our needs are usually at the bottom of a long list because we place others' needs before our own. Our careers are put on hold because babies don't keep.

You are a wonder, my friend. You are a wonder, woman.

When the enemy comes at you with bullets that try to destroy your true identity, his favorite weapon is a simple question: *Who do you think you are?*

Who Do You Think You Are?

Being women, we hear every opinion. We are told we are too much, not enough, that our value comes from what we do; we are told we are too loud, too quiet, too young, too old, too dumb, too heavy, too needy, too confident, or too insecure.

To do all that God has for us in this life, we have to know who we are. Our uncertainty about our identity is precisely why the enemy's question is so powerful. If he can make us question *that*— question who we are—then we will spend our time in confusion instead of walking in our calling.

But our calling is clear. We're not called to be people pleasers but God pleasers. We aren't called to give up when times get hard but to give in to God's will and draw strength from him. We aren't called to chase false idols but to chase after God.

You may not feel able to stand strong. You may be filled with self-doubt. When you hear others talk about great women of God, you may say, "Oh, that's not me."

But friend, it *is* you. You are more than you think you are.

A superpower exists inside you. If you are a believer, the Holy Spirit lives in you. We can't keep walking around feeling powerless, like life is happening to us, like we are victims. The spirit of God lives inside us, empowering us for greatness. We just have to tap into it.

You are worthy of salvation because he saved you. You are worthy of love because Jesus loves you. You are worthy of more in this world because he empowers you.

You no longer have the choice to say it's not you.

Being a great woman of God isn't about what you can do on your own. It's about standing strong in who you are in Christ and what he does in and through you. And that is good news. It means we can stop striving, because we aren't doing the work, God is. It means our pride is not on the line, because God is doing the work, so we can move out of the way and yield to him.

We can partner with God and press into the future he has for us, no matter what that looks like, no matter whom we work for, no matter where we live, no matter what.

Remember who you are. You are an *ezer*, a helper, a completer, an answer to problems.

You are a daughter of the king, filled with the Holy Spirit, believing the promise that God has created you and called you to stand strong in him. You are a wonder, woman.

I Want You to Remember

Women were not an afterthought to God. He created us last not because we are less-than but because we are the finishing touch.

Becoming a great woman of God is about allowing him to strengthen you *as you walk* into the next season of your life.

Being a great woman of God isn't about what you can do on your own. It's about standing strong in who you are in Christ and what he does in and through you.

Remember who you are. You are an *ezer*, a helper, a completer, an answer to problems.

You are a daughter of the king, filled with the Holy Spirit, believing the promise that God has created you and called you to stand strong in him. You are a wonder, woman.

Discussion Questions

1. What comes to mind when you think of a strong woman? Do *you* come to mind? Why or why not?
2. We, as women of God, aren't meant to buy into the false gospel of hustle and try harder. In what areas of your life do you feel pressured to hustle?
3. Our purpose is to know God. Our mission is to show God. In what ways are you getting to know God better? In what ways are you showing God to others?

Action Steps

Prayer: Ask God to open your eyes to see yourself as he sees you.

Journal: Ask God to reveal who you really are, and write it down. Place this list somewhere you can see it frequently. Refer to this identity statement whenever you are tempted to see yourself through the lens of your weaknesses, your struggles, or your limitations.

Practice: Think of a strong woman in your life. Someone is looking at you like that right now. Take a moment today to encourage another woman in her God-given strength. (For example, write a note, post a social media shout-out, or make a phone call.)

Part Two

What Holds You Back

On the journey to standing strong, we must break free from what has kept us stuck in the prison of self-doubt and fear for so long.

Let's dive into the places and obstacles that keep us stuck: when we think we're all we have and forget God's power, when we're afraid to disappoint others, when we don't feel supported, when we don't feel heard, when insecurity and doubt are loud, and when we listen to the wrong voices.

All these obstacles worked together to try to keep me from standing strong and moving forward to what God wanted for me. These experiences are the giants in the path to living with confidence. Every woman faces some or all of these giants at some point, and we all need the weapons—both spiritual and practical—to defeat them.

I don't know what you are going through right now or what God is calling you to do. But I know you can get through the valley, and you can carry out what is in your heart on the mountaintop.

Four

When You Forget Where Your Power Comes From

It's All Up to Me

I sat crisscross in my pj's on my unmade bed, with my phone in one hand and crumpled tissue in the other. My counselor, Amy, sat in silence on the other end of the line.

I could feel the words bubbling to the surface, along with the tears that waited to escape with them. For months I wasn't able to process all the thoughts swirling inside my brain. I hadn't talked through them with anyone, not even my husband. I know as well as the next person that speaking your thoughts makes them more real. Once they were out in the open, I knew I would be forced to reckon with them.

"God told me to leave my job," I blurted with a broken heave.

I had crossed the threshold. There would be no backtracking now, no keeping to myself and settling for the status quo.

For months that thought had been brewing inside me—in private and in darkness. It haunted my dreams and my daydreams. The thought of leaving my job and starting my coaching business over again from scratch seemed as easy as deciding to become a farmer and work the land—scary, somewhat stupid, and almost certainly destined for failure.

How could I leave my job on a Friday and then pop up on the web the next Monday and say, "I'm back! Please work with me." I help build companies for a living. I knew how long it can take. It's a process, and it takes time.

Not only that, but we had enough savings in the bank to keep us afloat for one month; that was it. And six mouths relied on me to put food on the table. Between the mortgage, bills, health insurance, braces, and school tuition, how would I cover it all? I couldn't see how I could walk away from the stability of a steady job and then in one month earn enough to provide.

Mark's going back to work wasn't an option either. His health was stabilized from his years of severe illness, but working a nine-to-five wasn't in the cards. For him to remain healthy, he needed specific lifestyle changes that precluded full-time employment.

One night I woke up just after four in the morning, sweating and shaking at the thought of losing everything again. We had survived bankruptcy and homelessness just nine years before, and I had promised myself I would never let us experience that again. It wasn't so much the house or the car or the loss of financial standing that had me frozen in fear. I knew Mark and I could handle it. As a couple, we thrive on chaos and crisis. When the world falls apart, we pull together.

But allowing my children to become collateral damage in the pursuit of my calling—there was no way I was going to let that happen.

I know the pain of growing up without resources. Of never once inviting a friend to my house because I was ashamed. Of not smiling because of my messed-up teeth while dreaming of one day having braces. Of not knowing if I would be okay. I didn't want that for my boys.

The thought of purposely putting my family at risk again made my stomach twist in knots. And most of all, I feared that if I told my family that God told me to leave my job and then I ruined our lives, they would blame God. That thought was overwhelming.

All my life, I just wanted to be a good mother. And this plan didn't feel like something a good mother would do.

A good mother provides a home filled with love, grace, and truth, but she also makes sure her children have the necessities of life. It's as if we are genetically encoded to know that good moms do not put their families at risk. Stepping off a cliff and saying, "God has called me to quit my job," triggered every maternal instinct I had to love, care for, and provide for my children. It felt too risky, which made me feel imprisoned between the tension of trusting God and trusting myself.

But as I sat there on the phone with Amy, I knew the time had come to release something that had been building up inside me. It was time to let it out, let it breathe, and face it head on.

This is a place you too have probably been—not sitting on the phone with your counselor but faced with a decision you know must be made and struggling to find the courage even to start the conversation.

Maybe it was telling your spouse you were ready to consider adoption after years of infertility. Or it was swirling thoughts about leaving your career to be a stay-at-home mom. Perhaps it was finding the courage to tell the one who is abusing you that enough is enough.

You knew it was a decision that came with a before and an after, and everything in the after would be forever different. But the time comes when you have to be brave, find your voice, and step out into the uncertainty.

"God told me to leave my job."

I was surprised at the freedom and relief that came with my confession. I don't think I fully realized the weight of the fear I carried until I blurted those words.

After Amy listened to my fears, she asked me a simple question: "Do you trust God to bring you enough income to support your family's needs after he told you to leave? Is God powerful enough to bring you what you need?"

Her question opened the floodgates.

I trusted God to save my soul, trusted that he was who he said he was, but deep in my heart, I didn't trust him to take care of me. And I definitely didn't trust him to take care of my family. In my mind, it was all on me. I was alone.

But I wasn't. God was there, waiting as he had always been. I had relied on myself and my strength and my hustle for so long that I lost the ability to trust others.

But sharing my anxiety with Amy—that small act of courage—taught me something. If we are going to remember who we really are and step out into a future God is calling us to, we have to partner with him in our new season. We have to say yes to the God who made us for more.

Partnering with God

If God were a college professor, every assignment would be a group project. If he were an athlete, he'd be the anchor of a four-man relay. If he were a southern breakfast, he'd be biscuits and gravy. And if he chose to be an animal, it would have to be a wolf, right? Because he loves to travel in packs.

God doesn't only like partnership, he *is* partnership. The essence of God exists in community: Father, Son, and Holy Spirit.

We partner with him to create things in the world he has given us. We create people, cultures, businesses, ministries, art, gardens, the wonder of dry shampoo—the examples of brilliant creation are endless.

God created this world and then created us to partner with him to fulfill his plans. He could have created us to blindly do his bidding. Or he could do everything without us. But he doesn't do either. He created us with personalities and the wills to make our own decisions because he wants us to join him.

I have a friend who has been a worship leader for twenty-five years. This year he invited his sixteen-year-old son to join him on stage to lead worship at a large camp. He didn't need his son on stage. He was perfectly capable of leading worship on his own. But imagine his pride and joy when his son joined him. Everyone in the room felt his love for his son in that moment.

That's why God invites us to join him. He doesn't need a partner. He could do everything without us. But he wants us to be a part of his story. That's our invitation. He is our God. Our Lord. He is not heavy-handed. He doesn't force his way into our hearts. He woos us to him. It is a dance of love and friendship.

God has beautiful plans for this world, both big and small—from technology that provides clean drinking water to millions to a backyard garden that provides

> **JUST AS GOD INVITES US TO BE IN RELATIONSHIP WITH HIM, HE INVITES US TO PARTNER WITH HIM.**

fresh blueberries to your family every summer. God has a plan for it all and invites us to join him in bringing it to life.

In Genesis 2, God creates the garden of Eden and tells Adam and Eve they have jobs to do. Humankind's first job was to work the land and take care of it. As God's partners, Adam and Eve were to subdue the earth, organize it, cultivate the land to grow crops, and raise livestock. Of course, their work changed over time, but all along, God intended them to be partners.

The garden of Eden was never planned to stay a simple garden;

it was designed to be transformed.[1] Don't you know God planned for our technological advances, our civilizations? He knew the day we would land on the moon, find a vaccine for polio, and create Amazon Prime free two-day shipping. He gave us the ability to work, the responsibility to rule over the earth, the wisdom to create, and the skills to build.

Just as our first ancestors were given the jobs of being fruitful and multiplying and working and taking care of the land, we are called to impact this world. It could be that you are an amazing teacher and manage your classroom with love and intention, or raise your children to love others well, or speak into the lives of nieces and nephews, or write a play that will change people's lives, or run for office and help protect your constituents through wise legislation.

You were made to do great work.

Sometimes your work shows up in the mundane and ordinary: comforting loved ones, filling out spreadsheets, washing dishes, or volunteering in your church or community. Your career as an insurance agent or a mother or an entrepreneur is vital to this world. It's kingdom work, and it's essential and holy because it makes the world a better place.

And a special note for those staying home with their kids. That was my career for ten years before I started my business. It is an important career choice; don't ever let anyone make you feel like the work you do is less important than work others do outside the home. You are living out God's calling through creating, teaching, and guiding the next generation. We need great women of God to raise kids who love the Lord, who have hearts for the vulnerable, who can give and receive love, and who work hard and take personal responsibility for themselves. You are showing up every day and saying yes to the greatness God has created you for.

You were created to partner with God by bringing his purposes to life in this world. The dream you have in your heart? He put it there because he chose you to partner with him to accomplish it. The skills and talents he gave you? They are there to fulfill his purposes on earth through you. And the ability to develop new skills throughout your lifetime? He put that ability there to allow you to adapt in each new season of life.

WE ARE CREATED TO BE GREAT WOMEN OF GOD AND TO DO GOD'S WORK RIGHT WHERE WE ARE.

You have to accept God's invitation to partner with him and move out of your own way to do it. We get in our own way because of fear, insecurity, lies we believe about ourselves, and lies we believe about God.

God was offering me an invitation to step into a new season of my life. He was patient and loving, and he was waiting for me to say yes to the future he was calling me to. I had to decide that my faith in him and trust in him were greater than any fear I had for my kids. I had to believe he was who he said he was and would do what he said he would do.

Maybe you have felt called to teach a Bible study, to mentor a younger coworker, to learn to fly-fish—something in your heart that keeps breaking the surface. That feeling could be God reminding you that he has more for you. But to get to that "more," you have to partner with him.

Partnership brings something new to life. A baby, a business, a book, a community group, an herb garden on your kitchen windowsill—each is something good, and each requires partnership to make it happen. God cares about the big and the little, the grand and the plain, the seen and the hidden. He has great plans for your life, and he is inviting you to partner with him to see it spring to life.

It took a partnership to create the world. God spoke the world into existence while the Spirit hovered over the water. And the ark would never have been built without a partnership of carpenters, right? The temple would never have been built without woodsmen and masons and stone workers, all partners in the divine. And Moses had a partner in Aaron in order to free the Israelites.

Even Jesus didn't want to do his ministry without a partnership of twelve men to walk with him on difficult days. Those same men also became a partnership of missionaries who went out into the world to build God's church.

When we think about the partnerships in the Bible, we see that God's story required partnerships to move it forward. **You are the newest link in this chain of partnerships that will carry the kingdom of God forward.**

I wonder if God asked anyone else to partner with him before Moses. What if we know Moses's story because he said yes but there were people before him who said no? How many people were asked to build the ark before Noah? How many people laughed it off and thought they ate some bad dates and brushed aside God's invitation to partner with him?

God doesn't force anything on us. He invites us to a future where we bring to life his plans and purposes for this world. God always has been, and always will be, looking for people to partner with his plans.

What if God planted the dream in your heart to bring his purposes to life in your sphere of influence?

This is a partnership mindset.

A Partnership Mindset

My friend Kelly, an amazing wife and mom of three girls, shared how a partnership mindset completely changed how she lived her life. Instead of automatically viewing her own dreams or ideas as selfish, she took them to God and asked him to make it clear which ones were from him. If they were from him, she asked him to bring resources to undertake those dreams, people to help her along the way, and encouragement to keep moving forward.

Years ago Kelly had a dream of learning to fly and getting her pilot's license. She felt like that aspiration was selfish because it would take time and money away from her family. But her dream persisted. So she asked God if flying was something he had for her. Feeling as though God was giving her the go-ahead, she discussed it with her husband, and he encouraged her to say yes to her dream, and they agreed to cut some nonessentials from the family budget to make her dream a reality.

Now, years later, with her girls in school, she not only has her license but also is an instructor and spends her days helping other people discover the joy of flying. Just imagine the delight she brings people every single day as they take flight.

What if you took your dreams and ideas to God, no matter how crazy or unlikely or outlandish they are? What if you asked him, "Lord, is this from you? If it is, bring me clarity, help me work this out, and give me the mentality to partner with you for what you want in this world."

Divine partnership is life's power source. But what does it look like to have a partnership mindset? Maybe the best way to explain it is to first examine what the opposite looks like.

A loner mindset says everything is up to me. It believes I am the hero of my story and destiny is in my hands alone. Live or die, succeed or fail, it's all on my shoulders. When life goes well, I take the credit and glory, and when it veers into a ditch, it's all my fault. I hustle for what I want, and I focus on myself. Living in a loner mindset is living in a desperate cycle of trying to accomplish in my own strength, experiencing failure, and then spiraling in disappointment. It sounds miserable and exhausting, doesn't it?

A partnership mindset says we are in this life together with God, living out his plans and his purposes in beautiful community. We don't have to be perfect or brilliant or particularly amazing at anything because God is the source of real power. All we are asked to do is show up and say yes to his invitation, do our part of the work, and walk strong in the knowledge that we aren't alone in this.

A partnership mindset means we know we have access to God for our resources. When life looks hopeless, we have a God who is near and provides just what we need. When our knowledge or abilities aren't up to the job, he gives supernatural gifts. This mindset understands that the spirit of God, the Holy Spirit, lives in us and brings wisdom, power, and strength every minute of every hour of each day.

For me, partnering with God meant deciding to trust him. And as I learned over the next year, it meant choosing to trust him over and over again every day.

We all have hurts and hang-ups that try to keep us from what we are meant to do in this world; they make it hard to trust and make playing small and having a loner mindset seem practical, so we have to decide every day to trust. We have to decide every day to partner with God.

Your life is part of a big beautiful story that you can't even begin to see the impact of. You may not know the full story until you're in heaven, when you discover how your work, your yeses, and your partnering with God changed the world.

> You may start a Bible study that changes your community for generations to come.
> You may raise a child who discovers a cure for a type of cancer—or teaches kindergarten, because Lord knows that's a calling.

You may help a woman rebuild her life after her marriage disintegrates in her hands.

You may write a book that comforts someone in a season of loss or inspires someone to run for president.

The world needs you to answer God's call.

No matter what season you are in, no matter how you have questioned God, no matter how often you believe you've messed it all up, or how many times you've said, "It's all up to me," God still wants to partner with you. He is continually calling you into your future.

You are not alone. You have the creator of the universe on your side. God is standing on the other side of the open door to the next season of your life. And in his hand is an invitation to a great adventure.

I Want You to Remember

Just as God invites us to be in relationship with him, he invites us to partner with him.

You were created to partner with God by bringing his purposes to life in this world. The dream you have in your heart? He put it there because he chose you to partner with him to accomplish it. The skill and talent he gave you? They are there to fulfill his purposes on the earth through you.

Partnership brings something new to life: a baby, a business, a book, a community group, or an herb garden on your kitchen windowsill. God cares about the big and the little, the grand and the plain, the seen and the hidden.

Your life is part of a big beautiful story that you can't even begin to see the impact of. You may not know the full story until you're in heaven, when you discover how your work, your yeses, and your partnering with God changed the world.

Discussion Questions

1. What dreams in your heart have you yet to explore?
2. When it comes to the dreams in your heart, do you have a partnership mindset or a loner mindset?
3. What fears pop up when you think about taking the next step into what you believe God has called you to do?

Action Steps

Prayer: Trust is the foundation of a healthy partnership. Ask God to reveal areas in which you have trusted yourself or others instead of trusting fully in him. Repent and invite him to be your source of strength in those areas.

Journal: Write down your wildest dreams (no matter how crazy, unlikely, or outlandish). For each one, ask, "Lord, is this from you? If it is, bring me clarity, help me to work this out, and give me the mentality to partner with you for what you want in this world." Write down God's response.

Practice: Next time you're stuck in a project or task, take a moment to invite God to partner with you on a solution.

Five

When You Are Afraid to Disappoint Others

I'm Letting Everyone Down

You know how when you forget to close a door or leave your dirty laundry on the floor, one of your wisecracking friends may remark, "Did you grow up in a barn?" Well, here's a little secret:

I may be the only person you know who can honestly respond, "Yes, I was raised in a barn, as a matter of fact." Seriously. My dad died in a car accident when I was almost three years old. My mother, who was only twenty-three years old at the time, spent the better part of the next year in a body cast recovering from the same wreck that stole her husband. My tiny body survived the accident somehow, a miracle that gave my mom hope, though she was grieving and penniless.

Lucky for us, my grandfather was in possession of—wait for it—a barn. With the help of my dad's friends, who were carpenters like he was, that old barn was transformed into a home for our family.

Our family friends often commented on the loveliness of that barn. They'd gush about the rough-sawn hardwood beams on the walls. I smiled and nodded in the polite way outlined in the unwritten etiquette manual that Southern girls know by heart. But inside, underneath the rough-sawn hardwood of my heart, I felt shame.

I dreamed of life in a suburban neighborhood with its warm red bricks, far from the country and its antiquated ways. I wanted smooth white walls like other families had, not rough planks with splinters that threatened passing hands. Something about drywall and wall-to-wall carpet conveyed security and belonging. I wanted the accoutrements of the families featured in all the eighties sitcoms I loved: a happy family and an adoring father who carried a leather briefcase and kissed my mother as he zipped out for work. I wanted a life that wasn't "different." But what I had was a painful, constant reminder of everything and everyone I didn't have.

You likely didn't grow up in a barn, but I bet something in your past or present has become a source of pain and shame. Your face turns crimson when anyone mentions it. You buried all the pictures of it at the bottom of a shoebox hidden on the top shelf of your closet. It represents all the ways you feel you are a disappointment.

I know, because I hid my shame in shoeboxes on shelves too.

My barn became a symbol of everything I didn't have and might never acquire, and yet it also became my home. Because my mother *made it so.* She battled her way through and out of debilitating depression. She constantly reminded me that I was loved and destined to be a great woman of God. My mother never let me forget that my future was mine and God's to make.

Finding the Root

If you ever find yourself at a party with a bunch of young Christians and you want to create a stir, ask them, "So what's an Enneagram, anyway?" The Enneagram has become a cultural craze even though it has existed for decades. I gave it a serious side-eye, chalking it up to the latest fad, but since reading up on it, it has become my new favorite personality profile.

According to the Enneagram, each person falls into one of nine main personality types. Some are reformers, some are helpers, some are achievers, some are individualists, some are investigators, some are loyalists, some are challengers, some are peacemakers, and some are like me. I'm a type seven, or "the enthusiast."

We are often known as the fun ones. Enthusiasts seek out adventure, jumping from project to project and idea to idea—the hummingbirds, if you will, drinking every drop of life's nectar. What moves and motivates people like me isn't the fun, or even the excitement of jumping from one thing to the next. What motivates us to seek out fun is our great need to avoid being stuck in pain. We fear being in situations where we are stuck in discomfort.

Enneagram experts say that ending up with a certain personality type is a combination of nurture and nature, which helped me recognize that the characteristics of my sevenness began early in life. As a little girl I spent too long as a victim of circumstances. As I grew, I avoided pain at all costs. I decided I would do everything I could to never again be stuck with what life handed me. What drove me at age ten tends to drive me to this day—I need options and I want choices. I need to feel empowered to change course or escape if necessary.

My feelings of shame and not being good enough intensified in middle school. My mom remarried and decided it was time to send me to the fancy prep school across town. Because it had a new financial aid program for poor students, it seemed like my mom's dream of a great education for me could be a reality.

Now, hear me when I say I am profoundly grateful my mom and stepfather sent me. The education was top-notch, the opportunities were broad, and my eyes were opened to possibilities in my life I couldn't have imagined before. But there was a downside: I was quickly hit with the feeling that I wasn't enough.

I couldn't compete academically; I was too far behind other kids my age. Our beat-up car and barn home that had seemed moderately acceptable to me brought shame when I saw how my peers lived. I was thankful for my uniform, which meant at least we were on the same level there.

I'll never forget my first month at school when I told some new friends I was excited to get carpet in my room that day. I had never had fluffy, soft carpet, just plywood floors. It felt like I was on my way to a normal life, like the girls I went to school with had. It felt like I was on my way to acceptance. "I'll finally be like all the other girls," I thought.

But I was wrong. Those eleven-year-old girls didn't accept me; they laughed in my face. In that moment, they realized I wasn't one of them, and they were angry I had even tried to pretend to be one of them.

Hot cheeks, shame, embarrassment, and regret came first. Later came the sting of disappointment. I was disappointed in myself, and I hated that I felt like a disappointment to them.

Isn't it crazy how a single moment can mark us with a lie that causes us to spend the rest of our lives trying to rediscover the truth.

The lie is different for each of us, but the pain is just as deep.

The lie could be from a parent whose harsh words made you feel like you'd never get it right. Or it could be a lie that left you feeling unwanted or rejected when you lost a parent early in life because of death or divorce.

The lie could be that someone from your childhood, maybe even a sibling, said you weren't pretty enough, thin enough, shapely enough, athletic enough, or smart enough.

The "sticks and stones" from kids in our childhood can wound us well into adulthood.

A counselor once told me that the fear of disappointing others can ultimately stem from tying love, worth, acceptance, and significance to the approval of others. The fear is actually not that we'll disappoint others. At the soul level, it's less about what we do and more about who we are; it's the fear of being abandoned, unloved, and rejected.

I've spent my entire adult life speaking truth to these lies of unworthiness. They are like the whack-a-mole arcade game. As soon as I hit one with a hammer of truth and it disappears, another one pops up. Through many years of tears, training, and trials, I've developed the strength to hit those lies with God's truth.

But no matter how many times I battle those lies, they keep popping up.

The fear of disappointing others is an enemy I've been wrestling ever since my daddy died. It has come up in different ways throughout the years, but at least I know now where it is rooted. Awareness of where our fears come from is the first step to removing their control over our emotions.

Facing the Fear

I pledged a sorority in college, which probably wasn't the best thing for a woman like me, who walked around always feeling "not enough" and like a disappointment. I quit just a month after I joined. I wanted to reject them before they could reject me—before I could be found out for being less-than.

Then, as a young wife and mom, I had a crash course in "normal" middle-class life, even though I worked so hard to fit in. When you grow up in the country in a literal barn, you miss some details.

I remember showing up to a "cookie party" and getting laughed at by the other moms because I brought a tray of store-bought treats instead of heirloom recipe snickerdoodles. Once again, I didn't measure up to expectations.

During my first year of marriage, a girlfriend told me a story of how she cleans when her mother-in-law visits, and she said, "It's time to bleach the baseboards." I asked what a baseboard was. We never had baseboards in the barn. It's a small, silly example, but it was another reminder that I wasn't normal. The lie that whispered how I was less-than and disappointing washed over me anew.

Through the years, I wrestled with God about my feelings of inadequacy and unworthiness. He replaced my vision of myself as flawed, less-than, and disappointing, with a vision of how *he* sees me: as his daughter, loved as I am and created to bring the kingdom all around me. We are all created in his image to expand the kingdom and do wonderful things in our spheres. The best part is that God's view of us has nothing to do with what we do; it's all because of his grace.

With much prayer and lots of counseling, I learned to calm that fear of disappointing others. For years it didn't play a part in my life. That is, until it was time to disappoint those I worked for and with. Then eleven-year-old Alli's feelings came flooding back into forty-one-year-old Alli's heart.

Because I believed my whole professional life was building up to working in ministry, I thought that was where I would stay. As I looked back, I thought giving up something great (a business) was for something even better (a ministry). I thought my business career was just a stepping-stone to a ministry career. It felt right; it felt good; it felt somehow holier.

But here I was, thinking about giving it all up. And I didn't even know why. Disappointment blindsided me.

For three years I had been trusted to steward the ministry's vision. The team I led and worked with felt like family, and we grew close through the years. Leaving them, combined with the fear of disappointing my family, was a weight on my shoulders that I thought would crush me.

The thought of letting everyone down gutted me. It was the same feeling I had the day I told my rich friends I was getting carpet. Shame. Embarrassment. Regret. Those feelings were familiar friends that came flooding back at the thought of abandoning my work family.

The fear of disappointing others does something to us, doesn't it? It makes the most confident of women second-guess themselves. It makes the strongest women play small and shrink back. It makes the wisest of women keep quiet and hold back.

What has the fear of disappointing others looked like in your life? Have you said yes to things you don't want to do because you're concerned about how you might look to others? Do you allow others to trample all over your boundaries because you worry people might see you as selfish if you protect your time and your family's time? Have you stayed in a relationship or a job because leaving might hurt someone else?

I think of Ashley, whom I met at a church event, hovering in the stage wings as she waited for me to wrap up my conversation. She caught my eye, and I knew she needed to talk. Ashley shared that she'd been in a relationship with a great guy for four years, but there was an element of their relationship she hoped would change: they didn't share the same faith. Ashley felt they needed to break up, but fear of disappointing him, her parents, their families, and mutual friends had kept her tethered to the wrong guy. In staying in that wrong relationship, she had cheated herself out of four years of living in the calling God created her for.

Like Ashley, I had to confront the way I used the fear of disappointing others as an excuse not to be fully who I was created to be.

But we can't let fear of disappointing other people keep us from our callings.

At face value, our choices that disappoint others seem selfish, hurtful, or even cruel. But let's look at this type of situation through a different lens.

Jesus is in Capernaum, a place he visits so often it's almost like a second home to him. He is doing what Jesus does: teaching with authority, healing people, casting out demons, and loving people in that town. Then change happens.

At daybreak, Jesus goes out to the countryside, hoping for a little alone time before the day's work is at hand. But the people of Capernaum look for him and find him. After he spends some time with them, they try to keep him from leaving. But he says, "I must proclaim the good news of the kingdom of God to the other towns also, because that is why I was sent" (Luke 4:43).

Picture for a minute that you are in the physical presence of Jesus. He has been sitting right beside you. You have heard him teach and watched him perform miracles, heal the sick, raise the dead, and feed the five thousand. Suddenly he up and says, "Well, y'all, I've got to get on down the road to my calling." How would you respond?

Sick, demonized, and hurting people were likely still in the crowd when he declared that it was time for him to go. There was still a lot of work to be done. I'm pretty sure the people of Capernaum felt disappointed when Jesus left.

Jesus disappointed people.

Let that sink in for a moment. Jesus, Word come to life, the right hand of God, disappointed good people who loved him.

Disappointing others is a natural part of living out our callings. No matter who we are, no matter where we are, no matter what we have been called to, there will always be more work to do. There will always be more people to serve, help, or encourage. When we are doing good work, work God has created us for and called us to, knowing that he may also call us to stop and move on can be crushing. Fear rises up in us, and we can't help but think, "What will people think of me if I just stop?"

The fear of disappointing others sinks into our hearts and minds and convinces us that surely a loving God would not call us away when much work is still to be done. Right? But we can't let our fear overcome our faith in the God who called us in the first place. We can trust that just as he is calling us to go, the work yet to be done is in his hands, not ours.

> **DISAPPOINTING OTHERS IS A NATURAL PART OF LIVING OUT YOUR CALLING.**

Sometimes living out our callings, walking in complete obedience to all God calls us to, requires us to be brave and push past our fear of disappointing others. I desperately wanted to obey. I wanted to be brave. I wanted to put on my cape and cross no-man's-land, but I had to face the fear of disappointing others once again.

How to Overcome the Fear of Disappointing Others

We can't navigate around the uncomfortable truth that sometimes living out our callings will end in disappointing others. This fear of disappointing others can lead us to stay stuck and, worse yet, keep us from fully stepping out into God's calling. When we feel tempted to fall into this trap, we must make two commitments: to stick to the season at hand and to challenge our thoughts.

Stick to the Season at Hand

Stay laser-focused on where God is calling you, and show up for the life he created you for.

A high school student who feels strongly called to go straight into a trade may disappoint her parents, who want her to get a higher education. A young married couple may disappoint relatives by moving to a different state for a job opportunity. A woman might disappoint her friends when she stops volunteering so she can devote her extra time to building a business. A mom may disappoint her child because she can't miss work to attend a school event.

These decisions are good and healthy. Yet saying yes or no to some things can disappoint or hurt others in the natural process of doing what we need to do in the season at hand.

What is your calling in this season? What dream is bubbling up in your heart that you want to pursue? Where do you feel God nudging your attention? Focus on your dream, focus on why it is important, and know it is healthy and good and okay to establish boundaries and make changes, even if that means your actions will disappoint people.

Challenge Your Thoughts

When we are afraid of letting others down, we play out situations in our mind, don't we? We imagine how people will feel, how they will respond, and how they will be let down. Often we imagine the worst-case scenario. We imagine the hurt, the anger, the judgment.

In my case, I imagined my colleagues angry. I imagined them feeling disappointed that I wasn't staying with the ministry I came to help build. I imagined my team feeling let down that I was leaving them. I looked at the situation through a filter of negative belief that produced a skewed reality.

When we are nervous about disappointing others, it's hard to see objectively, and we have to challenge our thoughts.

Say you are nervous about stepping down from a volunteer position because you don't want to let people down or leave them without help. Or maybe you are worried about telling your husband you feel called to put the kids in daycare and go back into the workforce. Maybe it's something as simple as not wanting to buy something at your friend's in-home party.

You have to ask yourself, "Am I afraid to disappoint this person because I'm afraid they will reject me? That they will leave me? They will talk badly about me to others? They will think I'm selfish?"

We need to know what drives us so we can shake off the habit of negative belief. We have to challenge our thoughts. We have to step back and say, "Is what I am speaking over myself true, or is it my fear talking? Is this idea rooted in fact or my feelings?"

When our minds run off and we find ourselves in an anxiety spiral, we have to step back and ask ourselves what is true and what is fact. You have to ask yourself, "Do I know this to be true?"

What I knew to be true was that Jesus had called me to leave that job, to face my fear of casting my family into chaos. I had to accept that disappointing others is a necessary part of living out my calling. The same is true for you. You must walk in your calling, even at the risk of disappointing others.

Your calling is unique and may change in each season. Your purpose in this life is simple; it is not hidden or hard. Your purpose will always be to know and love God and tell others about Jesus. But your calling is unique to you and the season you're in.

GOD HAS GREAT PLANS FOR YOU.

I might not know your calling in this season, but I do know that despite the disappointments you have felt, and despite the sting of disappointment from others, God has great plans for you. You have permission to disappoint others on the way to living out your calling. It's a natural, normal, and healthy part of doing what you are meant to do, of living the life you are meant to live. Sometimes disappointing others is what we are strengthened to do because it is necessary.

You are not a disappointment. You are God's *ezer*, a helper, a completer, an answer to problems. You can't find real happiness, real health, or real calling without sometimes disappointing others in the process. It does not mean you are selfish; it doesn't mean you are hurtful. It means you are living with purpose and intention. It means you are honoring the call God has put on your life. It means you are saying yes to the God who created you for more.

I Want You to Remember

We are sometimes called to do things that will disappoint others. Don't let this keep you from fully stepping out into God's calling.

Walking in complete obedience to all God calls us to requires us to be brave and push past our fear of disappointing others.

Stay laser-focused on God and his calling and establish good, healthy boundaries, even if it disappoints people.

You can't find real happiness, real health, or real calling without sometimes disappointing others in the process. It does not mean you are selfish; it doesn't mean you are hurtful. It means you are living with purpose and intention.

Discussion Questions

1. Is there a lie you feel like you've spent most of your life dismantling?

2. What has the fear of disappointing others looked like in your life?
3. We have to challenge our thoughts. Do you let truth or fear speak over you? Fact or feeling?

Action Steps

Prayer: Sticking to the season at hand is crucial to overcoming the fear of disappointing others. Bring this question to God in prayer: What is my calling in this season?

Journal: Make a list of both the blessings and the boundaries of your current season. If you become stuck, ask God to illuminate these for you.

Practice: Give yourself permission to disappoint others on the way to living out your calling.

Six

When You Feel Unsupported

I Feel Confused and On My Own

The air felt thick as I sat on the edge of my bed looking into Mark's eyes, trying my best not to say the words God was stirring in my heart. When I felt the urge rise, I'd change the subject or ask a question or pretend to have a coughing fit. But when I could hold them down no longer, the words flowed.

"Mark, I don't know what's next, but my time in this ministry is done."

Mark rose up on one elbow and stared at me. Clearly I'd gotten his attention. I continued.

"I don't know why God keeps leading me to new destinations only to tell me to pack up and move again. But I know it's time."

Confessing this to Mark was a relief because he had always been my filter to help decipher God's big messages.

In 2012, when God told me it was time to walk away from Blissdom, I wanted Mark to be my "out" and give me an excuse not to obey. After all, leaving Blissdom wasn't practical (Mark's strong suit), and he had just left his job at the hospital to focus on the boys because of my growing career. I thought Mark would be the bad guy who made the decision to ignore God's call. I'd just play the part of the "submissive wife." (Yes, I know, not my finest moment.) But Mark—my practical, reasonable, level-headed husband, my potential-way-out partner—replied that if God told me to leave Blissdom, I'd better hurry up and do it already.

Now with a similar message five years later, I felt confident I knew how the conversation would play out. Mark would tell me to follow God, just as he had before. And with his words, I'd find the confidence to finally rip the bandage off and do it.

Once my confession tumbled out, Mark looked at me with kind eyes and smiled. He stared at the floor for a moment and drew a deep breath. Then he leveled me: "After what we've been through, Alli, especially the last three years with this illness, we need stability. I don't think it's time to do this right now. God didn't tell you that you had to leave *now*, right? So let's wait until he tells you *when*."

I sat in stunned silence, nodding at Mark with the grimacing half-smile we always flash each other when our emotions get messy. Though I was surprised at his response, I was more shocked at how it made me feel. I wasn't mad or even disappointed. Instead, I felt relief. Deep down inside, in that cavern where we hide our secrets, I really didn't want to obey God this time.

Stalling felt like safety and, in the moment, like a gift.

Finding Your Team

Right after Mark quit his job to stay at home with our sons, he became severely ill with adult-onset asthma. For the next few years, he lived with a disease that kept him in and out of the hospital, struggling to breathe, and a few terrifying times he was near death. We spent years trying different medications for him, some that produced symptoms worse than the illness itself. We begged God to heal Mark and relieve us of the weight of constant panic.

My job wasn't only a source of income, it also afforded us great health insurance and paid time off. My coworkers were also my friends and formed a critical part of my support system. These benefits ensured I could care for Mark using my sick days and gave me the peace of not worrying about how to pay for ER visits. In a season of trauma and uncertainty, my job gave us some semblance of stability.

Conversely, life as an entrepreneur is risky. Some months are amazing, and others are tough. It is a fantastic experience full of freedom, but the ups and downs require a double dose of intestinal fortitude. I totally understood why practical Mark was pushing pause. His advice wasn't no; it was to wait until God told me when to leave. Though I didn't fully understand why we weren't both hearing the same thing from God, I felt relieved that I didn't have to carry the burden of shattering my family's sense of security again.

As the weeks crept by, my spirit slowly shifted. Everything in me told me to go. Each morning when I went to work, it felt like I was carrying a sack of potatoes around my neck. And the more I waited, the more the weight of disobedience pressed hard. As the months passed, I occasionally spoke to Mark again about leaving my job. Every time, he listened, smiled gently, and offered the same response.

"I just don't think it's time."

The ministry needed me, and our family needed stability, he would say before reminding me that we had just emerged from a season of hardship with his health.

Mark wasn't forbidding me from proceeding with my dreams. But he knew how much I trusted his opinion. Mark knows Jesus, and in the past, God had spoken to us separately, confirming big things in our lives. In this case, I chose to believe that if God was speaking to me, he would also speak the same message to my husband. When God's timing was right, we'd both know.

So I waited.

And waited.

And waited for my husband's heart to change.

As I waited, I chose to trust that God was working in Mark's heart. I tried to trust that God was honored by my waiting. But in that moment, the enemy's lie rang loud.

You don't have your husband's support.

When Others Don't Get It

There are seasons in life when we feel unsupported in our goals, when we feel called to something that doesn't make sense to others. We want their encouragement, but we also want their support and their wisdom. Have you experienced this? It might be that those closest to you don't get it or are even opposed to the dream building in your heart. You feel unsupported, confused, and alone.

Whenever I am faced with a significant decision, especially one requiring a leap of faith, I can expect three types of people to show up to the conversation: cheerleaders, naysayers, and slow adopters.

Challenge the Cheerleaders

I have a friend I seek out when I am frustrated about life— whether it's related to kids, work, or relationships. What I love most about her is that she says, "What do you need from me today? Are we mad, are we scared, are we over it?" She's a cheerleader. I can count on her for encouragement, even when we both know maybe I'm not thinking clearly about a subject.

Our cheerleaders are the people standing on the sidelines encouraging us to go for it, to risk it all, to live our lives, and to dream our dreams. They are the ones who make us believe we can have it all, do it all, and be it all, if that's what we want for ourselves. Having a cheerleader is important, yet it's equally significant to remember that sometimes rose-colored glasses cast a deceptive filter over the world.

Any time I have struggled to make a decision, my cheerleaders were there telling me to take that giant leap of faith. And with this big decision, they even went so far as to advise me not to let Mark "make me live in disobedience."

But I knew that wouldn't honor God.

I've spent enough years walking with God to know he isn't going to call me somewhere he won't lead Mark. It may take a while. It may not be pretty in the meantime, but if I was meant to leave, God would change Mark's feelings on the matter.

Your cheerleaders love you, and they want the best for you, but sometimes you have to challenge their advice.

We are naturally inclined toward people who tell us what we want to hear, even if it's not true. It's a phenomenon called confirmation bias. It means we tend to overvalue opinions and input that are consistent with our own. When people say we're great, we think, "It must be true because it rings true. They think I'm great. I think I'm great. I must be great."

It's important to filter their advice through God's Word and the leading of the Holy Spirit. The cheerleader's role is to cheer you on toward what you want, even if what you want isn't what you need. God gets the last word, not the cheerleader.

When your team is down by three touchdowns and there's a minute left in the game, the cheerleaders are the on sidelines acting like y'all still might win. It's good to have encouragers on your team. But it's important to balance their enthusiasm with a realistic look at what is happening on the field.

Nix the Naysayers

I'll be the first to say sometimes you need a naysayer in your life. Especially if you are an Enneagram 7 (like me) and you love thrill and adventure. Naysayers can bring a sobering reality to your life. However, naysayers also like to tell us why we can't do something without taking into consideration all the reasons we can. If naysayers were pro-wrestling triplets, they'd be Doom, Doubt, and Disaster because that's what they bring to the ring.

Maybe you're like my friend Jessica, and you have a dream of going back to school to be a teacher, but your naysayers tell you you're too old, it's too expensive, and you've worked too hard on your corporate career to give it up.

Or perhaps you're like the hundreds of women I've coached who desire to start a business, but their naysayers have made them doubt their idea, their talent, and even their sanity.

It could be that your naysayers have convinced you that stepping out in faith isn't faith at all—it's carelessness. They convince you that taking a risk doesn't honor God because if it were his will, it wouldn't feel risky. That's not only naysaying, it's spiritual manipulation.

Or maybe your naysayers are like mine: they have convinced you that if you follow God's voice, you are going to fail and it's all going to end in disaster—your dream will fail, your family will starve, and your kids will all grow up to hate God.

Doom.

Doubt.

Disaster.

Naysayers are like a body slam.

Jennie, a brilliant woman I coached through the years, struggled with naysayers. She had a dream to open a fitness center. It was years before she dared to share her dream with a group of friends.

Her dreams were shot down faster than a kid's request for a blowtorch.

One night with a group of girlfriends, she excitedly told them that she had a dream of opening a high-end studio and wellness center. It was as if she were announcing that she planned to ride a galloping unicorn over a rainbow bridge to Mars. Her friends laughed, and one sneered, "That's cute. But what do *you* know about business?"

You know that feeling when your cheeks are on fire, your eyes fill with tears, your chest hurts because your heart is racing, and you smile at the people who hurt you because you're confused and embarrassed and panicked all at once? Yes. That. Jennie was devastated.

Through coaching, prayer, and lots of healing, Jennie overcame what those naysayers spoke over her. She made the decision to believe in the dream God had put in her heart and push aside the lack of faith her friends showed.

Jennie told me recently that if she could do it over again, she wouldn't have announced her dream to that group of women. She would have nixed the naysayers and started with a coach, built her business plan, and then told a close friend or two.

Suffer the Slow Adopters

Finally, you'll encounter your slow adopters. The slow adopters are people who want the best for you but may not be the first ones to board the train to crazy town with you. You'll know them because they are the ones asking nine million questions, and for the life of you, you can't tell if they are for the idea or against it.

I say suffer the slow adopters because although you need cheerleaders (and naysayers too), you need slow adopters more than anyone else, even though their foot-dragging, question-asking ways will drive you crazy.

Slow adopters keep you from running headlong into a burning building until they are sure you are suited up for the fire. They keep you from swimming with sharks until they're assured you know how to dive and stay alive. And they don't let you jump out of a plane without checking your chute, twice.

Regarding my career decision, Mark was my slow adopter. His questions were practical, thorough, and relentless. But because I knew Mark's character and his relationship with God, I knew I could trust that God would align our hearts—in his time, not mine.

If you are married, you have to strike a balance between honoring what God calls you to do and honoring your husband's wishes. It is possible to do both, and it's important to do both. But how?

Every instruction and command from God carries blessing and life with it. That is for our benefit and for his glory (Deuteronomy 30:19–20). Jesus backed that up when he told us he would give us keys to his kingdom to unlock it here on earth (Matthew 16:19). Whenever we see a command in the Bible, we should ask, "What promise does this unlock?" For example, we can see in God's Word that faith unlocks salvation (Romans 5:2) and thanksgiving unlocks peace (Philippians 4:6–7). Submission unlocks order and security. When we submit to God's instruction to mutually submit to our spouses, order is released into our homes and lives. There is security in submission.

You may be asking, "But what if my husband is not submitting to Christ, as God also instructs?" Then you must entrust your husband to God, knowing you have security in your obedience. You can rest in knowing that your role as a partner with God is to obey his Word. God's role is to transform our lives. He will always accomplish his purpose (Isaiah 55:11). I want to be clear—this is in no way a license for any kind of marital abuse. God's Word is clear on this.

Slow adopters take longer than others to come around. In the meantime, pray that God will send voices of support and patience. Surround yourself with women who can help you strike that balance as you wait for God to move.

When a situation is complex and I don't know who to listen to, I filter the praise of my cheerleaders, the criticism of my naysayers, and the concerns of my slow adopters through the lens of God's Word (James 1:5).

OUR ROLE AS A PARTNER WITH GOD IS TO OBEY HIS WORD.

You don't need your friends, colleagues, or even your mom's permission or their understanding to do what God has put in your heart to do. Your gifts, talents, and dreams were placed there by God to accomplish his plans. He is the one who will grant you permission; he is the one who will always understand.

Some people won't get it. Some people will think you're crazy. Some will try to get you to go back to life before God started nudging your soul. Guess what? That's fine. They don't need to get it for you to do it.

Our culture may tell you that you can't achieve your dream because you're a woman, you've made too many mistakes, you don't have an expensive education, or you don't look a certain way.

Your own voice in your head may tell you that you can't do it.

Your friends may tell you that you aren't smart enough to build that business, holy enough (which is nonsense, by the way) to start that ministry, capable enough to foster a child who needs a home, or talented enough to go where your heart knows it's made to be.

Don't let someone else's limited opinion define your reality.

Say yes to what God places in your heart.

Pray that God will guide people in your life to support you in what you feel called to do.

And know it's not your job to convince the world that your calling is real.

It's your job to say yes and march with confidence into your divine destiny.

I Want You to Remember

Cheerleaders, naysayers, and slow adopters—each have value, and it's important to know how to take their advice.

Our role as a partner with God is to obey his Word.

Don't let someone else's limited opinion define your reality.

It's not your job to convince the world that your calling is real.

It's your job to say yes and march with confidence into your divine destiny.

Discussion Questions

1. Who are your cheerleaders, naysayers, and slow adopters?
2. Have you let someone else's limited opinion define your reality?
3. What are some ways you have supported others in following their dreams?

Action Steps

Prayer: Confess to God the times when you have felt unsupported in your goals. Ask him to heal your heart from any hurt, bitterness, or unforgiveness. Pray that he will work in the hearts of the important people in your life to support you in what you feel called to do. Invite him to expand your capacity to hear his voice and follow his lead.

Journal: Write down the comments from others that surface in your mind when you try to step forward into your calling. Is there a theme? Do you dwell mostly on negative comments? Do you remember the praise as clearly as the criticism? Filter the praise of your cheerleaders, the criticism of your naysayers, and the concerns of your slow adopters through the lens of God's Word. Ask God for wisdom on how to receive praise and respond to criticism and doubts.

Practice: Find a way today to support a friend in following her dream or living out her calling.

Seven

When You Have Lost Your Voice

No One Understands Me

I would have made the world's worst pioneer mother. Amazon Prime is as essential to my life as a good night's sleep, and who can live without steaming services like Netflix? Not me. I shudder to imagine life without toilet paper, air conditioning, or Google. I don't know how our ancestors survived without the ability to manage problems and answer questions with the click of a few keystrokes.

How to get your colicky baby to fall asleep? Hand me my phone.

Want to know what a brontosaurus ate? Got it covered.

Should I worry about the weird rash crawling up my kid's armpit? Be right back.

Of course, motherhood is a rough road despite these advancements. Having children can transform us into humbled, exhausted, yet superhuman versions of ourselves. From the lack of sleep and years spent singing along to toddler music to dealing with your kids' bad breakouts and bad breakups, motherhood is filled with finding strength we didn't know we had, wrestling fears we didn't know existed, and sacrificing dreams we never voiced.

When Mark fell ill, I had spent almost fifteen years building

91

my strength as the primary caretaker to our tribe of boys. I assumed I was prepared for almost any trial life could muster. After all, we had already survived financial failure, building a business from the ground up, and the truly horrific perils of puberty-induced mood swings. How difficult could adult-onset asthma be? But when Mark's illness became life-threatening, I learned exactly how difficult life could get.

I found myself in the middle of the scariest storm of my life. Years passed by in a blur of doctors, sleepless nights, and worries bolstered by the weight of accumulating medical bills. I could have been crowned the queen of compartmentalization and sat tall on my throne of emergency management. When a breathing crisis arrived unannounced, I calmly doled out Mark's medication while hooking him up to his nebulizer. Turning on a dime, I'd then stroll into the living room, turn on a movie for the boys, and glide into the kitchen to whip up a snack—all with a smile that would make a Disney princess envious. But inside, I was suffocating from my own fear.

Then after three-and-a-half years of illness, the failed medicines miraculously started working. Mark entered what the doctors called remission and we called a miracle. With a quiet fear that his illness would return at any moment, Mark began the battle to rebuild his health. He still needed ongoing medicines and specific lifestyle changes, but for the first time in years, Mark was well.

My constant fear that his lungs would fail him and I would lose him forever was lifted. Life was healed, whole, and headed in the right direction.

I needed a break for once, and I'd earned it. I looked forward to a season of security with space to heal from the trauma I'd been through. And somehow God thought this was the perfect moment to tell me to leave my job and step off the cliff into another abyss of uncertainty. Sure, my life made me tough and brave, but this vision for my future felt like a bad joke.

"My friends at church don't have to go through this," I thought. "They're all so happy with steady jobs and normal lives. They get stressed over traffic, carpool lines, and the amount of playing time the little league coach gives their child."

I felt a low-grade, almost constant, seething anger under the surface. I constantly questioned God and was jealous of other people's seemingly comfortable and steady lives.

"Why can't I have a normal life like everyone else? Can't I just get a break? Why do I have to have a roller-coaster life?"

I reminded God of my suffering.

"I'm the one who's had a sick husband for years. I'm the one who has obeyed and given up so much. Why am I the one who has to constantly put our security and comfort on the line?"

I rejected God's plan in favor of my comfort.

It's a slippery slope from asking God why to telling God how to solve your problems.

"This can all wait."

So when Mark told me to wait before leaving my job, I exhaled relief.

Have you ever found yourself here, questioning God, reminding him of all you've endured? Have you ever chosen human comfort over divine destiny?

Time to Fight

It was September, a little over a year after Mark's medication had begun to work and his healing began, and I developed a cough and a few headaches. They were nothing more than an annoyance. But by early October, my hacking cough was with me day and night.

The doctor treated me for acute bronchitis and gave me prescriptions, which I imagined would cure me by later that week.

I had never been so wrong.

The next week my voice became little more than a whisper, while the tightness in my chest tried to convince me I was having a heart attack. The specialists were stumped, and for the next several weeks, I sat through test after inconclusive test. The specialists agreed that I needed rest.

My primary care doctor identified that my stress levels were off the charts, and he suspected stress was the reason my body couldn't fight what was attacking it. I wanted to laugh at the suggestion. His diagnosis was so absurd, I wondered if he was also secretly googling my symptoms or consulting Siri for answers. Stress . . . really? That's the best he could come up with? Even more hysterical than his diagnosis was his prescription: "Alli, you've got to rest and reduce your stress."

"And how would you suggest I go about that?" I laughed to cover the tension of my reply, but I was furious. How could rest and destressing be the answer? Ridiculous! After all, Mark was well. What did I have to be stressed about?

And once again, my seething anger found its way to the surface, this time showing me exactly what was stressing me out. I knew deep down there was a war being waged between what I wanted and what God desired. Living in constant disobedience to his will was affecting every part of my life, health included.

God was calling me to speak, to teach, to coach others, and I had lost my voice. The irony was not lost on me.

Eastern doctors often say that when one loses their voice, it's a sign of a deeper, spiritual reality. The loss of a physical voice is the body's way of telling us that we've lost our metaphorical voice. It's a sign that we are struggling to speak up and speak out. I can't confirm their notions, but my pain and bouts of coughing were sure trying to tell me something.

The constant coughing kept me from sleeping. I slept propped up in a recliner or on pillows, but only for an hour or two at a time. One night the combination of my cough and my pain woke me up at three o'clock in the morning, and after a session of coughing, crying, and feeling sorry for myself, I cried out to Jesus.

Jesus, Jesus, Jesus, Jesus. Tell me what to do.

He responded to my spirit.

Do what I taught you and fight.

The previous two years of my life had been spent writing *Fierce Faith* while Mark was sick. I wrote battle plans to fight fear with step-by-step instructions on what to do to overcome anxiety and worry. But in my pain and despair, I had forgotten it all. The weight of life seemed to have crushed my will, and I forgot that fighting was even an option.

I had to be reminded not to give up, reminded that I was not going to be beaten by this, reminded that I was not alone, and reminded that God had not abandoned me.

In the pain, both physical and emotional, I had lost touch with my voice and that mysterious inner strength that can overcome anything—strength from God.

In that dark room in the middle of the night, God could have healed me. In a millisecond, the cough could have vanished, my chest could have stopped causing unrelenting pain, and my voice could have returned. But he chose not to heal me in that moment.

Sometimes instead of healing us instantly, God calls us to fight.

He calls us to fight through our anger.

He calls us to fight through our disappointment.

He calls us to fight through our bitterness.

He calls us to fight through our fear.

He calls us to fight our way to forgiveness.

And in fighting, we become familiar with our hidden strength that has been there all along.

My battle in that season was resisting the urge to quit and give in to despair. I veered dangerously close to believing I would be sick with this mystery illness forever and living life as a victim of it. Instead, I fought. Waging this war meant new doctors, new tests, new medicines, and a new diet. It also meant taking care of myself for the first time since Mark had fallen ill years earlier.

I sought out traditional and alternative medicine. I took handfuls of vitamins, lathered in essential oil potions, and flushed my sinus cavities with a neti pot. I did it all.

God wasn't calling me to give up. He was calling me to fight, as God does with us all.

Called to Fight

I don't know what your fight is, but I know you have one. To live on this earth means to fight in some way.

Maybe it's praying for that crazy-making coworker who makes you want to kick her in the shins.

Maybe your battle is little more than crawling out of bed when you'd rather pull the covers over your head and sleep until noon.

Is your fight asking God to restore your love for the man you married?

It could be making that phone call to get help for the mental health issue you keep ignoring.

Or maybe, like me, your fight is embracing your most honest, authentic self and finding your voice again.

Whatever your battle may be, remember your battle buddies. Just as God uses cheerleaders, naysayers, and slow adopters to speak to you, he will also send you battle buddies. These are the special friends who will crouch beside you in the foxhole while you fight. They'll pray for you, build back your confidence when you are weak, and remind you of who you are called to be.

I don't know what I would have done without my friends Bianca, Carol, and Stephanie in that season. You need to identify those people in your life too. Invest in your battle buddies. Build new relationships and strengthen existing ones with people who are loyal, fearless, and wise. And if you can't seem to locate any good candidates, then step out in faith and become the type of friend you want. One of the New Testament's most foundational principles is that we reap what we sow (Galatians 6:7). Sow a friendship seed and wait for the harvest of community to follow.

There are going to be seasons of your life when friendship is abundant and other times when it may seem sparse, but you can rest in this truth—you always have the Holy Spirit as your friend and counselor. Jesus said the Holy Spirit is our helper and will guide us in all truth (John 14:25–26).

If I were sitting with you now, talking about how we will fight, I would pour you a cup of coffee and lean in close and tell you what I believe God wants you to know.

He wants you to know . . .

Your blessing is coming, but right now you need to fight.*

Your breakthrough is coming, but right now, daughter, you must fight.

Fight for your life, fight for your joy, fight for your voice, fight for the woman God created you to be, fight for the future he has for you.

The enemy will put up obstacle after obstacle along the way to steal, kill, and destroy that future. An illness, a broken relationship, a job loss, or a struggle with mental health can leave us stuck

---

* Just to be clear, by *blessing* I don't mean you're going to win the lottery or inherit a million dollars from that great aunt you didn't know you had. I mean the peace, strength, comfort, security, and rest you long for.

in despair and ready to abandon hope. And without hope, we can't fathom that we are able to fight.

Maybe life experiences have weighed you down so heavily that you feel like you lost your voice and your power long ago. They seem like just a distant memory. But God has plans for you, there is strength in your future, and you are reading these words right now because it's time to connect with God. He will help you find your voice, and he will give you the strength and power to fight.

Finding Your Voice

Esther is the patron saint of the voiceless. She reminds us what it means to speak up, even when we think we can't. Esther's story opens with her being taken from her home to become a part of the harem of a powerful, albeit foolish, king. Fueled by rage over his queen's refusal to attend a drunken party, the king had banished the queen and ordered all the beautiful virgins of the land to be rounded up, dressed up, and stored away for later use.

Esther is an orphan living with her cousin, a Jewish man who submits to the king's order, sending Esther to a seemingly dark, unspeakable future. What must go through her mind as time passes and she waits to be called to her inevitable service to the king?

Does she ever think about escape?

Does she ever wonder where God is, what he's doing?

Why doesn't her cousin fight for her?

Why doesn't she fight for herself?

Perhaps the greatest mystery to Esther was the parting words of her cousin who said, "Don't tell anyone you're a Jew."

Stripped of her identity and hidden in obscurity, Esther lost it all—her family, her home, her identity, and her voice. She must have spent countless months praying and thinking, "Can anyone hear me? Does anyone care what has become of me?" Years pass and Esther becomes queen, deeply loved by the king. But still she does not speak of her home or her heritage.

Then one day she discovers the king has been duped by his most trusted advisor, Haman, into ordering all the Jews in his kingdom killed. The words of her cousin, Mordecai, echo in her ears: "Don't tell anyone you're a Jew."

Stunned, she sends for Mordecai, who sends her this message: "Do not think that because you are in the king's house you alone of all the Jews will escape. For if you remain silent at this time, relief and deliverance for the Jews will arise from another place, but you and your father's family will perish. And who knows but that you have come to your royal position for such a time as this?" (Esther 4:13–14).

Esther, having waited years to see God's plan unfold, plans the perfect moment to unravel Haman's plot before the king. She asks, "If I have found favor with you, Your Majesty, and if it pleases you, grant me my life—this is my petition. And spare my people—this is my request" (Esther 7:3).

God uses her to speak in such a way that she saves the entire nation of Israel.

Wow. Talk about standing strong and finding your voice.

When the circumstances in your life overwhelm you, know that God is working in the background.

Seek his wisdom, be who he is calling you to be in the waiting, and then speak.

Just like Esther, we face seasons of uncertainty. We are uncertain of ourselves, uncertain of our dreams, and uncertain of God's plans. Pray that God will bring clarity. We see all throughout Scripture that he hears us when we call, he is with us, and he will not abandon us, even though at times we may feel like he has. If you feel beaten down, lost, and like you don't have passion for anything anymore, ask God for clarity.

Ask him to show you where he is working.

Ask him what your fight is in this season.

For Esther, her fight was coming; she was in a season of preparation. Sometimes just being reminded that God is building us, strengthening us, and preparing us for our future is exactly the clarity we need.

Get Up and Live

Esther lived a life she never would have chosen for herself, but trusting and waiting on God to reveal his plan, she fought and finally found a way to be true to her authentic self.

Created to be a queen and a rescuer of her people, Esther found a way through hell to be a hero. Just like Wonder Woman crossing no-man's-land, Esther waited for her moment.

Maybe Esther didn't know what greatness God had planned for her, but she knew the greatness of the God she served. So every day, she made the choice to get up and live.

And when it was time, in God's time, she found her voice. And so will you.

We don't all have the same story. I lost my physical voice. And because of that, I lost my sense of calling and the trust I had in the greatness of God's plan. As I wallowed in the waiting, I forgot to live, truly live, and I forgot to fight.

DON'T WALLOW IN THE WAITING.

Maybe that's you today. You feel like God is calling you to more, but nothing in your life supports that. You have no idea what God is doing. His plans don't seem to make any sense, and you're tired of waiting.

We have all been there. It's easy to wallow in the waiting.

But like Esther, we can hold fast to our identity as strong women of God. We are daughters and sisters and friends and wives and mothers, and the fight is in us. Our voice is still there. And at the right moment, guided by his plan, we will speak.

Maybe you are in a season of uncertainty, with circumstances far outside your control, and you're not in a position to change anything.

It could be that your husband has lost his job, and your dream of quitting your own job and homeschooling the kids has been put on hold.

Or you have a loved one whose life is in crisis, so you need to help them instead of chasing your dream right now.

It could be that you are in a toxic friendship that needs to end, but getting out of it creates drama you don't want to deal with.

Or maybe, like me, you're being called away from something you love, and the uncertainty of that is staggering.

It may feel like you have no power over your circumstances right now. But sister, don't let your current reality trick you into thinking God doesn't have a plan. His plan for your life is not limited by your current situation.

Pray.

Trust God.

Keep taking those steps every day toward your future.

Keep fighting the fight in front of you.

Get up and live.

In the right season, you'll find your voice, and when you find it, you will be heard.

I Want You to Remember

Whatever your battle may be, remember your battle buddies, the special friends who will crouch beside you in the foxhole while you fight. They'll pray for you, build back your confidence when you are weak, and remind you of who you are called to be.

Fight for your life, fight for your joy, fight for your voice, fight for the woman God created you to be, and fight for the future he has for you. The future he created for you requires your partnership.

God has plans for you, there is strength in your future, and you are reading these words right now because it's time to connect with God.

His plan for your life is not limited by your current situation.

Discussion Questions

1. It's a slippery slope from asking God *why* you have problems to telling God *how* to solve them. What is your current prayer posture? Are you entrusting your burdens to God or telling him how best to solve your problems?
2. Sometimes instead of healing us instantly, God calls us to fight. Are you in a season in which you believe God is calling you to fight? If so, what are you fighting for right now?
3. Like Esther, we must hold fast to the truth that we are strong women of God, even when life seems out of control. What truth are you speaking over your life and circumstances?

Action Steps

Prayer: Ask God to show you where he is working. Ask him what your fight is in this season. Be sure to wait and listen. Trust him to speak to you. When circumstances in your life overwhelm you, know that God is working in the background.

Journal: Writing is a great practice for those who are finding their voice. Schedule time to write about what's on your mind without putting pressure on yourself to make it perfect. If you are in a situation where you haven't felt you had a voice to speak up for yourself, practice what you want to say in your journaling time.

Practice: Choose one of your battle buddies whom you feel safe sharing your message with. It doesn't have to be formal; it could be a casual conversation. If you are practicing how to speak up for yourself, be sure to get feedback from your friend. Does it resonate? Is it clear? Loving feedback given by a battle buddy can help you develop clarity and confidence as you develop your voice.

Eight

When Insecurity and Doubt Are Loud

I Don't Have What It Takes

If you ask any dog whisperer, they will tell you that dogs have this crazy sixth sense. I have friends who say that when they are sick, their dog is a constant companion. I know this is true because it's something I experienced with Mollie, our golden retriever.

As I walked through this season of being sick and feeling frustrated with my calling, I remember Mollie following me around the house, clinging closer to me than the clothes on my back.

Everywhere I turned, there she was.

If I reached down to pick up the newspaper, there she was, panting in my face. If I walked across the room, I'd hear the pitter-patter of her paws behind me. She was there by my side for every trip to the kitchen to reheat my tea, and she sat at my feet whenever I read in my study.

One morning, I woke up early and nearly broke my ankle trying not to step on her as she lay cuddled up close to the side of my bed.

I wondered what was wrong with her.

Was she sick?

Was she in pain?

Was she trying to tell me something by keeping close to me?

Then, slowly but surely, I realized Mollie wasn't the one in trouble.

I was.

Mollie followed me around because she sensed that something in me, something I had not even yet recognized in myself, was not okay.

I was at rock bottom. I felt alone, unsupported, disappointed, and frustrated about what God was asking me to do. And now I was sick. I felt helpless and stuck, unable to escape a reality that threatened to overtake my heart and mind. I went through each day in a daze, often ending up in a room in my house wondering why I'd walked in there in the first place. Mollie was following me around because she sensed my despair, and she whined her grief alongside mine.

I was drifting, completely untethered to any sense of security or control.

My cough was my constant companion. I coughed so much I almost had abs. (And you know that after I've had five babies, the only thing that keeps my stomach tight is Spanx.) All day long I coughed, sleeping for only an hour or so at a time. The more I tried to talk, the more I coughed. My herbal tea collection expanded into a second cabinet, and the other moms at school teased me that they never saw me without a giant mug of hot tea and a purse full of tissue and cough drops. I smiled and nodded. I lost the will even to attempt a sassy reply since I would only fall into a coughing attack anyway.

I begged God to show me it would all be okay. I knew I would go back to my work as a business coach. Consulting and coaching are second nature to me. It's as easy as breathing. It's as though God has given me this innate ability to walk someone through strategy and leadership skills and, at the same time, speak into their life and spiritual growth. But I knew that wasn't all I was meant to do in the next season of my life.

When I repeatedly asked God what was next, he said one word over and over again. Every question had the same answer.

Preach.

What in the world? I must be hearing him wrong.

How could *that* be the answer? Didn't God see what I was going through? I was sick, Mark still wasn't on board with me leaving my job, and my voice was gone. The cough had stolen my ability to communicate more than a few sentences at a time for the last few months. How could "preach" possibly be God's answer when his plans depended on the one element I was missing—the ability to communicate?

The Magic Wand

I love challenging my coaching clients with a "magic wand exercise" to help them identify their goals and dreams. I ask a simple question that always unlocks clarity.

"If you had a magic wand and life could look exactly like you want it to in twelve months, what would it look like?"

Dreams and goals become crystal clear within minutes.

Jordan from Tacoma dreams of starting a business where she coaches twenty-somethings to find career success.

Taylor from Dallas wants her company to sponsor and organize a 5K.

Stephanie from Mobile hopes to write a book and double her speaking engagements.

Jennifer from Saint Paul wants to double her income and work fewer hours.

Allison from Orlando plans to start a ministry for foster parents.

And Erin from Phoenix wants to sell her business and retire in Hawaii.

Once we wave the magic wand and they put their dreams and goals out there, we make a plan, filled with clear action steps, to do just that.

One Monday evening, seemingly out of the blue (isn't it funny how God's nudging always seems out of the blue in the moment), I thought, "Maybe I should take my advice and coach myself."

I made my way to the kitchen and grabbed a giant mug of hot tea, my journal, and my favorite pen and got started. In that moment, I glimpsed light amid the darkness. If I could coach my clients through their uncertainty, surely I could do the same for myself. Right?

I started to write.

- I want to start a podcast to learn from friends and coach people on life, faith, and business.
- I want to start accepting speaking engagements that I have had to turn down the past few years while I have been employed.
- I want to rebuild my coaching business and help business owners lead well and enjoy their work.
- I want to help as many women as I can bring their God-given dreams to life.

The exercise felt right. I felt strong, in control, ready to tackle my goals like Wonder Woman crossing no-man's-land. I stood up and held my journal to my chest as I walked over to the big window that overlooks my backyard. I smiled and breathed in what felt like the biggest, deepest breath I'd taken in months.

Then the familiar feeling of self-doubt crept in, along with its companion, despair. What was I thinking? I couldn't accomplish my goals because they depended on being able to use the voice I had lost.

My lungs tightened again. I prayed one more time and said, "God, what do you want me to do?"

And still, God's only answer to my gut-wrenching prayer was *preach*.

God's response of *preach* had frightened and confused me.

Naturally, it brought thoughts of a formal church ministry and pulpit preaching. But for the first time ever, I wondered if it encompassed more.

Was God really calling voiceless me to be a voice of goodness and love? To preach to his daughters about living life abundantly, growing in confidence, and accomplishing the things he calls us to do? Could preaching mean simply sharing my story—telling women about the gift of freedom and the grace of standing strong?

It was as if he was saying, "Preach of my goodness. Preach of my love. Preach on how to live life abundantly. Preach on how to grow and build and accomplish great things. Preach on your story. Preach about freedom. Preach and tell women to stand strong. Preach!"

Yet I was voiceless.

One sunny Sunday, Mark was napping, and the boys were being independent like older boys are—watching football, playing video games, playing with the dog. They were all distracted. I went into my room and locked the door and knelt on the floor, placing my face on the carpet, and begged God to heal me.

I promised God that if he gave me my voice back, I would use it for his glory the rest of my days. The tears soaked the carpet, and my voice tumbled out in whispers and whimpers. I half hoped my voice would surge strong and powerful by the time I reached amen. I mean, that's the way miracles occur in the Bible.

A blind man's sight was healed with spit and mud.

A paralyzed man was healed with a dip in a pool of water.

The bleeding woman was healed by touching the hem of Jesus's road-worn tunic.

I expected my voice to erupt so loudly that my guys would burst through the door, shouting alongside me as we all witnessed my miraculous healing. Instead, I began to cough again. Tears of begging morphed into tears from coughing. There I was on the floor, gagging and gasping. I found my nearby mug of hot tea, propped myself up on my bed, and felt sorry for myself.

Once the coughing subsided, I called Carol. When God doesn't make sense to me, when self-doubt doesn't allow me to believe what I hear God say, she's my phone-a-friend. I asked, "How can I even begin to make plans for whatever future is in front of me when I hear God calling me to an impossible task? Why won't God heal me?"

Carol responded, "Alli, what if God has already healed you but your fear of what lies ahead is silencing you?"

Our conversation fell quiet.

She wasn't saying that my fear was keeping me from being healed. She was asking if maybe my fear was keeping me from realizing he had *already healed me* and I needed to give the process time.

In the years since that phone call, I've known countless women who are standing on the edge of an unknown future, much like I was. They know they are meant for something else, something more than they can see, but the circumstances of their life keep them mired in doubt.

I'm not saying for one second that God hasn't healed you because of self-doubt or because of something you have or haven't done. I don't believe God works that way. We can't let our limited perspectives put artificial limits and barriers around all God can and will do. Instead, I'm telling you to reach through your doubt and your fear and believe that God is a God who works in the mystery of what we cannot see.

An Impossible Reality

A few months before my illness set in, I spoke at a women's event and led weekend services at the host church—the Saturday night service and three services on Sunday morning. In the weeks leading up to my teaching at the church, I convinced myself that I was absolutely not qualified to lead their weekend services. I thought of calling them and canceling my speaking at the weekend services 7,456 times, roughly. You name the excuse, and I practiced it.

"I can't take this much time away from my family."

"I broke my leg."

"My needy dog wants me back home Saturday afternoon."

Was I honored to have the chance to teach God's Word to thousands of people? Honored beyond words.

Did I have a desire to take on such a responsibility? Absolutely not.

Was I sure I would throw up sometime between service two and three? Without a doubt.

I could have convinced them of the broken leg, but no way were they going to buy the golden retriever bit. Obviously, I couldn't break one of God's top ten no-no's and lie my way out of it.

Despite my overwhelming self-doubt, I was driven by a promise I made to God years ago: "Whatever you call me to do to serve the local church, I will do."

I couldn't say no.

A few weeks after the conference, I was once again curled up begging God to give me some clarity when I received a call from the church. I assumed the call would be about me returning for their women's conference the next year. I love speaking at conferences and meeting women from all over the country, so I was a little surprised when the call went in a completely different direction.

The pastor didn't ask me back for the next year. Instead, he asked me to join the teaching team and teach a few times a year.

Self-doubt crept in and walloped me. I rattled off in my brain all the reasons I shouldn't do it: I was a woman, I wasn't qualified, I hadn't been to seminary, no one would listen to me. Then I remembered my promise to God to always accept the call to serve the local church, so I ignored my self-doubt and accepted on the spot.

But how could I now fulfill my commitment to preach when I coughed continually and had all but lost my voice? I had said yes when the pastor called, but inside I was still saying no.

Self-Doubt, the Killer of Dreams

My biggest problem wasn't Mark's saying wait to leave, it wasn't my coughing fits, and it wasn't my lack of voice; it was me.

My real problem was self-doubt.

God had told me what he wanted. God had all of it handled, whether I chose to believe him or not. God had told me what to do. Leave. He had given me a clue as to what I was going to do when I left. Preach.

What I lacked was any belief I could be successful in this new venture.

The trauma of Mark's years of being sick, the misery of my illness, the fear of messing up my kids' lives, the memory of losing all we owned a decade before—it all added to me feeling like I couldn't do it.

I spiraled in a sea of self-doubt. My mind was relentless as it asked one punishing, self-doubting question after another.

Will I ever get better?

Will my voice return?

Will I cough so much that I can't talk to my clients?

Will I start a new podcast and then have to go on hiatus when I lose my voice again?

Will I travel to speak at women's conferences and live in fear that my voice won't hold up?

Will I ever be able to do all God is calling me to do?

All those goals on the list I had so confidently compiled? My insecurity and self-doubt convinced me they were dreams I would never achieve.

That's the way of self-doubt. It is the silent serial killer of dreams.

Self-doubt makes us drop out of college because we probably wouldn't finish anyway. It keeps us from applying for that dream job because someone else is probably better qualified. It tells us to stay quiet and play small at work because our ideas might be shot down. It convinces us not to take a chance on a new relationship or end one that needs to stop.

Self-doubt causes us to question ourselves over and over until we are paralyzed.

Self-doubt is fed by our feelings. And our feelings are about as stable as a three-year-old bingeing on Pixy Stix.

Have you ever decided you are going to wake up early and go to the gym or read your Bible?

What happened when your alarm went off? If you are like the rest of the world, you didn't feel like getting out of that warm bed, and you didn't take action. Sure, having a morning quiet time or getting in shape is what we want. But when the alarm goes off, we don't feel like getting out of bed, and we don't change our behavior.

Why is that? **It's because we make decisions and take action based on our feelings in a split second instead of making decisions based on wisdom and truth.** Wisdom is what we know to be true in our minds, and truth is what we know from God.

My feelings were getting the best of me. I was disappointed

that I had to sacrifice what I loved—the conference, the ministry (what would I have to leave next?)—and angry that my health had disintegrated. My feelings made a tough situation unbearable. I couldn't get out of my head or out of my way.

Isn't that what we all do sometimes?

The bad news comes, and our foundation feels rocked.

The diagnosis comes, and we lash out at God, asking where he is in all this.

The betrayal occurs, and we feel like life will not go on.

The report card comes home, and we believe we've failed as a parent.

Feelings are important. Feelings are good. They are healthy. God gave them to us. We feel happiness when we see our dog after a long day away and joy when we hold a baby. There's sadness when we feel loss, and anger when we recognize injustice. And we feel horror when we realize we have to use the bathroom at a gas station while wearing a romper.

OUR FAITH KEEPS US FOCUSED ON THE FUTURE.

OUR FEELINGS CAN KEEP US STUCK IN OUR CIRCUMSTANCES.

Feelings are to be listened to, examined, and enjoyed, but the moment we let our feelings make decisions for us without the accompanying voice of wisdom and truth, we're done for. If we let our feelings run wild, we end up amputating our leg because of a broken toe.

My feelings overshadowed what I knew to be true. I knew God was telling me to go. I knew he told me it would be okay. And I knew my calling was to preach: to preach his goodness, to preach truth, to preach freedom. But where my faith would keep me focused on the future, my feelings kept me stuck in the wilderness of my present circumstances. That's exactly where I was—stuck in the wilderness, unable to believe God was calling me to a promised land just ahead.

I wanted to take steps to prepare for what I felt called to do. I wanted to research how to podcast. I wanted to take a few Saturdays and begin drawing up plans to relaunch my business. I wanted to do some of the important foundation work. But I didn't *feel* like it.

The Five-Second Secret

Forced to take a couple of weeks off from work on sick leave, I devoured books, Bible studies, and magazines in a way I hadn't had time to in years. Without the ability to talk, I focused on learning. In one book, I learned about a simple way to trick your brain into taking action instead of making a split-second decision based on your feelings.[1] Because our brains are hardwired to keep us from danger—or trying to do difficult tasks—when we get in the habit of hesitating, our brains say, "Well, let's not do this after all."

When something feels uncomfortable, when we hesitate instead of doing what we planned to do and know we should do, our brain stops us. At the heart of every moment is a choice to take action or not. We make split-second decisions to step away from fear and self-doubt and step into our goals, our dreams, and our future—or not.

It all happens in a couple of seconds, five seconds to be exact. Now, as a mom of all boys, I felt pretty confident I understood the five-second rule. If you drop a chicken nugget on the ground, you have five seconds to pick it up and eat it before the dog gets it, before it's too dirty to eat, or before one of your brothers beats you to it. You don't stop to think about it; you just go for it before your brain (and common sense, in most cases) talks you out of it.

Oddly enough, my understanding wasn't that far off. Part of the brain is called the prefrontal cortex. It controls our decision-making, self-control, planning, goal setting, and whether or not we should eat the chicken nugget that fell on the floor—basically all the stuff we do as adults.

We can outsmart our prefrontal cortex by saying, "Five, four, three, two, one, go!" So when our brain tells us, "Nah, I'm going to stay in bed/keep quiet/eat that third donut/text that ex because I'm lonely," we can develop a five-second mantra to override our bossy brain.

Here's what's amazing: it worked. In my season of low-key depression with my illness, it helped to get up early when I wanted to pull the covers over my head. When I wanted to waste hours on social media, I reminded myself to use the free time to invest in myself. The five-second rule, counting down from five, was so simple, but it felt a little flat and powerless to me. So I made a prefrontal-cortex-tricking system (that's an "Alli technical term") that changed my life.

As a woman of God, I know I can stand strong for one reason: God. We are powerful because of God. We have unlimited, unseen resources available to us because of God. Our wisdom, help, purpose, and gifts are all because of God. Not because of what we do but because of who he is.

I needed God. I needed to partner with him to overcome the self-doubt, the lack of inertia, and the heartache. So instead of a simple five-second countdown, I changed it from the five-second rule to the five-second secret. I said a simple verse. "I can do all things because Christ gives me the strength [Philippians 4:13 NLV]. Five, four, three, two, one, go." I can do all things because Jesus, the secret sauce to life, gives me strength.

When I wanted to hit snooze because it would be another day of pain, I thought, "I can do all things because Christ gives me the strength. Five, four, three, two, one, go." And I would get up out of that warm, soft bed.

When I wanted to go eat a pint of chocolate almond ice cream and watch Netflix for hours instead of doing the Bible study I finally had time to do, I said, "I can do all things because Christ gives me the strength. Five, four, three, two, one, go." (And you know I treated myself with that ice cream and movie afterward.)

When I wanted to stay stuck in my present wilderness instead of taking microsteps toward the future in faith, I said, "I can do all things because Christ gives me the strength. Here I go."

It was so simple. So effective. So life-changing.

When we bring God into any battle, we win. When we partner with God even on the tiny decisions we make throughout the day, we walk away from the wilderness and toward the future. We walk away from the lies that we are all alone, that we aren't taken care of, that we aren't enough.

When you bring God into the little things and let his Spirit help you push past self-doubt, you honor the calling he has on your life.

Strong and Confident

I was taught that courage isn't the absence of fear; it's the willingness to face your fear. Confidence doesn't mean we don't have self-doubt; it means we push forward, take action, and do what we need to until we no longer doubt.

Have you ever believed confidence is something we either have or don't have? Just like some of us have curly hair, brown eyes, or a third nipple, some people seem to be born with confidence. But here's the truth—confidence is not something we're born with; it's something we build.

Confidence is a skill that must be built up over time, and the only way to do that is by taking action.

You learn to ride a bike first on a tricycle, then with training wheels. Then we become so skilled at the training wheels that one falls off and we don't even notice. Then we become brave, take off the training wheels, and go for it, wobbling down the road (and probably wiping out a few times along the way). Sometimes the process takes years, tears, and lots of skinned knees. But what results is confidence. You suck it up, take action, practice, manage your fear, and go for it, even if you wobble and wreck a few times.

It's time to shed self-doubt and step confidently into your calling.

What does God want done that he is asking you to help him with?

Is his heart broken because of the injustice of trafficking, and he put the dream in your heart to raise money to fight it? Does he want the second grade children in your town to have a loving teacher to develop them, and he nudged you to apply for the job? Does he want a local business to thrive so the owners can continue doing good in the community, and he wants you to pitch yourself as the new marketing person?

God called us all to do good works—not to earn our salvation, not to earn his love, not to prove we are worthy but because he loves us, saves us, and gives us new hearts to love others.

God delights in partnering with you for his purposes, and it's time you believed that. You're not an evil villain plotting to take over the world; you're a woman of God partnering with him to make the world right here and right now a better place.

When Jesus spoke of the kingdom in the Gospels, he was also talking about the here and now, not just in heaven. What does God want to do with you in his kingdom here and now?

Whether you're delivering comfort food to a grieving family, rocking a baby in the nursery, folding laundry and praying for a friend, growing a garden that feeds your family, or growing a non-profit that feeds the world, it all matters to God. And it is work that builds the kingdom right here.

He wants me and you and all of us to get over our self-doubt and start living the lives he created us to live. And that starts with the small decisions we make every day.

When you want to say to yourself, "I can't do this," and self-doubt tries to sideline you, remember.

Remember who you are.

Remember where your strength comes from.

Remember that you are a wonder, woman.

Remember, you are called to stand strong.

So start standing.

I Want You to Remember

When we bring God into any battle, we win.

When you bring God into the little things and let his Spirit help you push past self-doubt, you honor the calling he has on your life.

As women of God, we can stand strong for one reason: God. Our wisdom, help, purpose, and gifts are all because of God.

Confidence is a skill that must be built up over time, and the only way we do that is by taking action.

Getting over self-doubt and living the lives God created us to live starts with the small decisions we make every day.

Discussion Questions

1. What specific self-doubts arise when you start to step into what God has called you to do?

2. Do your current self-doubts overshadow what you know to be true?

3. Do you believe confidence is a trait you either have or don't have, or do you believe it is a skill that can be built over time?

Action Steps

Prayer: Confidence is a skill that has to be built up over time, and the only way we do it is by taking action. The first step is to decide to think differently about who God is and who you are. Worship is a great way to renew your mind. Throw on your favorite worship album, and spend time praising God for who he is. Think about his attributes (for example, faithful, loving, strong, kind). Allow who God is to overshadow any self-doubt.

Journal: If you had a magic wand and life could look exactly like you want it to in twelve months, what would it look like? Write it down. Then ask, "God, what do you want me to do?"

Practice: We make split-second decisions to step away from fear and self-doubt and step into our goals, our dreams, and our future—or not. Develop your own "five-second mantra" to override your bossy brain.

Nine

When You Listen to
the Wrong Voices

They Said I Was a Failure

One Thursday afternoon, my friend Bianca called to tell me I was just like one of Jesus's favorite disciples. Unfortunately, she didn't mean it as a compliment.

"Alli, I know this sounds crazy, but I just taught on Peter, and when I was finished, God told me it was a message for you," she said.

I'm usually suspicious when somebody tells me *they* have a word from God for *me*, but Bianca is wise and measured, and she's not one to take this lightly.

"You are like Peter. You don't have any faith," Bianca said. "God wants me to tell you that you wrote a book about fear, but you are too scared to trust him. He wants you to get out of the boat."

Womp. Womp.

She was right. Or rather, God was right. I was stuck between the sure footing of what was and the unknown of what was yet to come. I was too beaten down by my insecurity to take action, too sick to believe change was possible, and too scared to have much faith.

God had told me what he wanted, and I ignored him. When I finally confessed this to Mark, he advised me to wait. Then I got sick.

And sicker. Now, months later, here I was, a mess physically, mentally, and spiritually. And in the process, I'd forgotten how to trust God. I stopped listening to my friends because their advice conflicted. Some said go, some said stay, some said wait, some said I needed to pray more, and some said I needed to stop praying and start doing.

After hanging up the phone, I did what many people do after hearing from God: I tried to convince myself that it never happened. Staring out the window, I imagined all the ways that Bianca's revelation could be coincidence. Bianca knew I was dragging my feet to obey God, sure. And she knew I had just finished writing a book about fear. I wanted her to be wrong.

Then the next call came.

It was my friend Carol, and she jumped right in just like Bianca had.

"Hey, I know this sounds crazy, but stay with me," Carol said. "I think God wants me to ask you if you believe what you wrote in *Fierce Faith*. Or are you afraid to trust him?"

In that moment the air shifted, and I knew I could no longer pretend. One call should have been enough, but God knows how stubborn I am. So God sent two messengers to speak an identical word to make sure I heard him clearly. That brought me to my knees.

"Dear God," I said. "I'm afraid. I'm afraid to trust and afraid to obey and afraid to move on. Help me get over this need to control, this need to know it will be okay, and help me trust you enough to step out into the future you've made for me."

This wasn't all I prayed. I asked God to change Mark's heart. I prayed for miraculous healing from my head down to my toes. I cried out to God every night, wrestling sleep and often fighting tears.

To get to the future that was waiting for me, I had to trust God. I had to take those terrifying first steps and prepare for a future I couldn't see.

Even as my mind found peace in the understanding that I *could* trust God, my body found new ways to betray that trust. I had a procedure done to test for ulcers, and the doctors developed a new treatment plan for my seemingly unending medical problems. R & R was part of the doctors' treatment plan. During my days of recovery, I read great books, binge-watched TV, and dove into a new Bible study. And once again, God showed up through the voice of a friend.

Bianca called again to check on me. And in true Bianca fashion, she didn't pull any punches just because I was sick. She is one of those people who, if she feels she is getting instruction from God, will drop everything right there and obey. She doesn't question, delay, deny, or make excuses like I do. The wrestling I do with God is unfathomable to her.

She was checking up to see if I had made a decision and was taking action. I gave her my well-practiced reasons why I wasn't: I'm recovering from surgery, Mark still says wait, and I don't want to.

"Alli, God didn't say you could stay. I believe you are relying on other people because you don't trust yourself. Girl, you need to get a God word. The enemy is going to put fear in front of everything that brings God glory. I need you to live the words you wrote in *Fierce Faith*. Walking away doesn't make sense to you now, but it's going to make sense when you do it. It's sackcloth and ashes time. Get on your knees, hear his words, and get in his Word for confirmation. Dare him to back it up in Scripture."

Later I prayed and felt silly. I had absorbed some of Bianca's fire and was hoping for Jesus to float down into the room to talk to me. But I prayed and didn't hear anything. I didn't feel any different. I started wondering what fabric sackcloth was made of and where I could find enough ashes to cover myself.

I went back to my couch with the built-in recliner and snuggled back into my recovery station. I had my hot tea, enough blankets for an army in January, my Bible, my laptop, a journal, and three books all half read and marked up. I wasn't going anywhere.

I turned on the Bible study video and was listening half-heartedly as I skimmed a book when the teacher mentioned the book of Numbers. I felt God nudge me to listen. She mentioned the book of Numbers again, and God said, "Go read that right now."

Numbers? Really? How Numbers was related to my current situation, I had no clue. And at this point, racked with self-doubt, I no longer trusted myself to hear anything correctly, from God or anyone else.

Regardless, I turned to the book of Numbers and read.

Numbers focuses on Moses and the people of Israel *after* they'd been delivered from Egypt.

At the age of eighty, Moses found himself the leader of the Israelite nation. Delivered from slavery in Egypt, the Israelites wandered the wilderness, still under God's continual care. (God literally dropped food out of the sky to feed the people.)

And even though he took care of their every need, they continued to mess up.

As Moses was getting the Ten Commandments from God, the Israelites melted their jewelry, made their own idol, and worshipped it. It was a cow. A ridiculously ordinary cow. God provided manna. They demanded meat. Moses's siblings, Miriam and Aaron, complained to God so loudly about Moses that God struck Miriam with leprosy for seven days. God showed the Israelites a land flowing with milk and honey, but all they saw were the giants in the land. God took them to the edge of the promised land, and they complained about being thirsty.

I started to see a theme.

God provided.

They complained. And I believe they got scared and doubted. That is why they took matters into their own hands.

Over and over and over again.

And then it happened.

God told Moses to *speak* to a rock and water would pour out of it, providing the Israelites, once again, with all they needed. But when Moses arrived, he was so done with their behavior that he said (Alli Living Translation), "Look you bunch of knuckle-heads, do I have to do everything?" Then he *struck* the rock and water came out—and Moses was forever banished from the promised land.

God said, "Because you did not trust in me enough to honor me as holy in the sight of the Israelites, you will not bring this community into the land I give them" (Numbers 20:12).

God wasn't asking me to talk to a rock that day. He brought me to that passage to read a story of a person whom God loved and whom God was patient with. Moses was a friend of God who said yes to partnering with God but missed out on God's best for him because of his disobedience.

In that moment, I felt afraid of God. Not afraid because God was mean or unjust but because I was willfully doing wrong. Like Moses and all the Israelites, I got scared, doubted, and continually complained and took matters into my own hands. God, who is kind, fair, loving, and slow to anger, was showing me where I was headed if I continued. He whispered, "Don't miss what I have for you because of your unbelief and distrust."

I had a choice to make, and the rest of my life hung in the balance.

I sat on my blanket-filled recovery couch and wept. I didn't need the sackcloth and ashes after all. I wept for how I had hurt God and how I was hurting myself, and then I wept out of relief that I had made the decision, finally, to trust him.

Just then Mark came through the front door and saw me and said, "What happened to you?" I said, "It's time. I have to go." I didn't bother to explain about the rock and the water or Moses; Mark could see on my face it was time. We couldn't deny it any longer.

I refused to sit on the edge of the future God was promising me. It was time to stop being afraid, stop doubting, and start listening to the one voice that mattered.

Your Worst Critic

The most debilitating critic in your life is not the person you assume it is. It's not your nasty boss, your backstabbing coworker, your pessimistic best friend, or your mother who hasn't found a way to believe in you since you were in grade school. These people are problematic and can hold you back. *But the most dangerous critic is the one living inside you.*

She knows you better than anyone and always has the perfect barb to cut you off at the knees. The inner critic doesn't care about being honest; she cares about keeping you from doing anything that might allow you to fail. Unconcerned with trusting God, the inner critic worships the pantheon of false gods of security, perfectionism, and acceptance. An unholy trinity if ever there was one.

Your inner critic consumes all your thoughts, all your focus, and all your trust. On the one hand, she tells you that you must control what happens in your life and trust only yourself and your instincts. She just as quickly reminds you that you aren't smart enough, strong enough, well enough, or wise enough to accomplish much.

And if that doesn't work, she tells you that you aren't godly enough to be called to anything.

Your inner critic is so constant you might not even notice her. She's been whispering lies to your soul for so long, you begin to wonder if maybe the voice you hear is the Holy Spirit guiding you, and that's where the deception begins. Your inner critic is not the Holy Spirit. The roots of your inner critic go all the way back to the garden where Eve was tempted.

"Now the serpent was more crafty than any of the wild animals the LORD God had made. He said to the woman, 'Did God really say, "You must not eat from any tree in the garden"?'" (Genesis 3:1).

And just like that, Eve doubted what God had said, believed the enemy's lies, took matters into her own hands, and forever changed the face of humanity.

We can even convince ourselves that our inner critic is good for us, that she wants what is best for us: It's not that she doesn't want us to succeed; she doesn't want us to fail. It's not that she doesn't want us to go for that promotion; it's that she doesn't want us to put ourselves out there and be told we aren't good enough. It's not that she doesn't want us to pray for healing; she just doesn't want us to be disappointed when God doesn't keep his promises.

> **THE MOST DANGEROUS CRITIC IS THE ONE LIVING INSIDE YOU.**

But those are lies. Your inner critic is like a mentally unstable nanny screaming at you to stay safe while continually tearing you down in the process. And her voice is just as dangerous as the liar that spoke to the first woman in the garden.

The inner critic says:

- You can't do anything right.
- You are a terrible mom.
- You always ruin everything.
- You're so stupid.
- You'll never be happy.
- No one can really love you.
- You will always be a failure.
- God didn't tell you that.

She is so convincing that if you allow it, she shames you into submission and self-doubt.

Shame is a feeling that you are inherently flawed. It induces thoughts such as "You're so stupid" as opposed to "Well, that was a stupid thing to do." Notice the difference? Shame says you are stupid, that you are flawed, instead of focusing on something you did that maybe was stupid or flawed.

We all engage in stupid behaviors. Give me an hour; I'll probably do something dumb in that time span.

When we mess up, we are supposed to feel bad. That's called guilt. We need to feel guilt and remorse because it causes us to repent and seek forgiveness. We need to reconcile if we have hurt someone, but then we need to leave it in the past.

Healthy guilt drives us to repentance, which is beneficial. Shame doesn't work that way.

Research has shown that shame does not make us change our behavior for the better, whether we shame ourselves or try to use shame to change someone else's behavior. Rather, it causes hurt.

We don't have to give our shaming inner critic a seat at the table. We can learn to recognize her, reject her lies, and with trusting faith, silence her.

After those two prophetic phone calls in one day, I realized I had spent too long listening to my fear and to the voices of those around me who confirmed my fear. And just between us, I liked listening to them because it made me feel like I didn't have to obey. I had wrapped myself in a blanket of self-doubt and ignored God for as long as I could.

And then I heard God ask, "Alli, who are you listening to?"

Mark wasn't holding me back. He was a convenient excuse. The voice that was holding me back was me.

How would you answer God's question?

Who are you listening to?

The Voices That Speak into Our Lives

I had four sets of voices in my life: God asking me to trust him and take the first step, my friends and family who encouraged me to wait, others who thought I was crazy for thinking God would call me away from something so incredible, and my inner critic and fear telling me I was too sick, too scared, and too unprepared to do what God was asking,

I needed to choose which voices would control my destiny, just like your responsibility is to choose the voices you listen to.

Another voice in our lives can be just as dangerous as the people we know well—the voice of social media. It's staggering how much value we place on the voices speaking to us through social media, often through people we hardly know. We are called to dwell in the secret place (Psalm 91), not on the screen in front of our face. But often we let the success and pace of others set our pace, regardless of what the Holy Spirit tells us. We should never let a catchphrase replace the voice of God in our lives.

Sometimes life is noisy and our filters become weak, making it hard to determine exactly whom and what we are hearing.

> NEVER LET A CATCHPHRASE REPLACE THE VOICE OF GOD IN YOUR LIFE.

A friend of mine was recently telling me about a visitor she had in her home. One day, when she thought she was home alone, she heard a weird scratching noise. She craned her head sideways to try to hear it better, and just as quickly the sound was gone. She made a mental note to ask her kids if they'd ever heard it, but moments later they came busting through the door from school, and any thoughts she had of asking them about the scratching sound were soon drowned out by the sheer force of their volume.

Later, at dinner, as she paused to pray, she heard the sound again. Midprayer, she yelled, "Do you hear that?" They all started talking at once, and she said, "Quiet! Now listen." Sure enough, they heard it. Like silent soldiers, they scoured every inch of their house trying to find the source of the noise. Finally, they discovered it was a squirrel in their attic that had gotten in from faulty flashing on their roof. Judging from the size of the nest, the exterminator said the squirrel had been there a while and brought friends. But the family had never heard the squirrels because everything else in their house had crowded out the sound of them.

That's the way it is sometimes. God is there in the background, trying to be heard above all the competing voices in our lives. He says, "I'm here. I've got something pretty big going on over here for you. Can you hear me?"

Maybe he whispers inaudibly to your spirit. Maybe he sends you visual pictures of the future. Maybe he sends you to a certain part of the Bible and uses the words to come alive and speak to your situation. And maybe he sends fellow believers to confirm what he has spoken to you in private.

But with the hectic pace of our lives, sometimes telling the difference between our voice, the voices of our family and friends, and the voice of God is hard. Because I almost missed God's voice completely, I have learned to ask myself the following questions when I'm trying to discern his voice above all else:

Is it loving?
Does it invite me to love him more, love myself, and love others?
Am I being encouraged to step out in faith?
Am I being shamed into submission or encouraged in obedience?
Am I being led to stay small or enlarge my faith?

God always gently calls us to more. **He opens doors, he brings new understanding, and he makes us uncomfortable today in preparation for the new thing he is preparing us for tomorrow.**

For you to step into that new thing, he asks that you learn to listen to him, that you listen to the voices that align with him, and most of all that you decide to partner with him.

It is your responsibility, and yours alone, to guard yourself against the wrong voices, whether they are from within or without. It's your responsibility to actively partner with God to stand strong, overcome your inner critic, and live with the confidence to hear and trust his voice.

He has created you to be a great woman of God, the completion of all creation, called, anointed, gifted, and filled with the Holy Spirit. What he's asking for is your heart, your trust, and your yes.

I Want You to Remember

The most dangerous critic is the one living inside you. The inner critic doesn't trust God; she worships the false gods of security, perfectionism, and acceptance.

Your inner critic has been whispering lies to your soul for so long, you begin to wonder if maybe the voice you hear is the Holy Spirit guiding you, and that's where the deception begins.

The inner critic is a liar. She's like a mentally unstable nanny screaming at you to stay safe while continually tearing you down in the process.

We don't have to give our shaming inner critic a seat at the table. We can learn to recognize her, reject her lies, and with trusting faith, silence her.

It's your responsibility to actively partner with God to stand strong, overcome your inner critic, and live with the confidence to hear and trust his voice.

Discussion Questions

1. Are you afraid to trust God? If so, why?
2. When making a decision or searching for clarity, where do you go for feedback? Do you go to God as much as you go to others?
3. Sometimes life is noisy and our filters become weak, making it difficult to determine exactly whom and what we are hearing. Not all noise can be avoided (like busy toddlers or demanding jobs), but what noise can you start reducing today? For example, social media and extracurricular activities.

Action Steps

Prayer: What voices have you been listening to? Ask God to speak above the noise of all the other voices. Ask him to make your spiritual ears sensitive to his voice.

Journal: Sometimes telling the difference between your voice, the voices of your family and friends, and the voice of God is hard. Write down what you sense God is telling you. Then ask these questions:

- Is it loving?
- Does it invite me to love him more, love myself, and love others?

- Am I being encouraged to step out in faith?
- Am I being shamed into submission or encouraged in obedience?
- Am I being led to stay small or to enlarge my faith?

Practice: Never let a catchy tweet replace the voice of God in your life. Take inventory of your weekly input (for example, TV, social media, books, friends, church, time with God). Where do you receive the most input from? Do these inputs encourage you in living your calling? If not, fast from them for a week. After the fast, take note of any difference in your mindset, emotions, and overall countenance. Ask yourself if it's worth reintroducing those inputs.

Part Three

How to Move Forward with Confidence

Here we go. We've battled our way through the giants in our path that try to keep us stuck. We've explored what scares us and what slows us down, and we've learned to overcome them with God's strength.

We made it to the fun part! Let's explore the six keys to moving forward with confidence. As great women of God, we have the power of prayer, obedience, courage, belief, authenticity, and community.

You are an *ezer*, a helper, a completer, an answer to problems. You were designed with purpose to create, complement, and complete. Let's unlock the six keys that are needed to step into the future with strength.

Ten

Ask for It

I'm Relearning How Prayer Really Works

The day I had dreaded for months arrived, and I walked into the meeting to announce my departure, unsure of how my well-prepared monologue would go. I was still a mess, still sick, and still desperately hoping God was going to step in at the last minute and tell me it was all a test. Yes, I was walking in obedience, but it was much the same way my middle schoolers walk when they are asked to carry something upstairs—resentfully, one heavy footstep in front of the next.

Even with all the preparations and my determination to be mature and professional, halfway through my well-crafted talking points, the tears slipped out. I loved my work, my team, and the leadership I served under, and I was walking away from it all.

By the end of the meeting, we had a transition plan in place, and my fate was sealed. That sounds so ominous, like I was doomed in some way. I wasn't. I was walking by faith where I couldn't see a road. But even though my comfort was in a God who is steadfastly the same yesterday, today, and tomorrow, my worry never eased up.

We agreed that I would continue my role for three months so the transition would be smooth. During that time, my church partnered with a seminary to allow church members to take evening classes. I signed up for Systematic Theology. I mean, come on. It seemed like the perfect next step for a depressed, voiceless, God-told-me-to-preach Baptist female.

As we went around the room on the first night, introducing ourselves to the class and saying why we were there, I realized I wasn't even sure why I was there. When it came my turn to speak, I whispered with a cough and a rasp, "Hi, y'all, I'm Alli. I share about what Jesus is doing in my life, and I want to make sure I'm not committing accidental heresy."

I was there, in the beginning at least, only to get more of God. Everything in my life felt out of control, and a class named Systematic Theology sounded like just the tightly bound structure I needed. I needed to calm my nerves, be assured I was really hearing from God, and to know for certain I wasn't going to hurt my family or their faith.

Every Wednesday night, there I was with my Bible, my books, a giant thermos of hot tea, and a purse full of cough drops. I knew the class would be a great distraction from my worry, but what I didn't expect was how much I would fall in love with theology and the many undiscovered truths that had sat under my nose my entire Christian life.

Discovering Truth

Theology is the study of God. And theology isn't only for people who feel academically inclined, it's not just for those who want to be in the ministry, and it's not for people who feel somehow worthy to study. Theology is crucial for every believer to live the abundant life Jesus talked about in John 10:10.

A. W. Tozer said, "What comes into our minds when we think about God is the most important thing about us."[1] Our theology matters because how we view God determines how we live our lives. Will we choose bravery or fear, love or hate? Will we find the strength to forgive or take the easy route and let bitterness fill our hearts? Will we believe what God says is true and walk by faith in that, or will we choose our own path, controlling our own destiny?

God led me to that theology class to show me, in a new way, his heart for me, his heart for you, his heart for all his people. When we learn more of who he is and how he loves us, our lives open up to the unseen resources and the miraculous adventure that is wrapped up in him.

> **HOW WE VIEW GOD DETERMINES HOW WE LIVE OUR LIVES.**

Unseen Resources

It's not easy to admit this to you, but I forget to pray. I've always felt God loves me and known he was intimately involved in the details of my life, but I forget he wants me to talk to him. I know he knows my thoughts and the intent of my heart and has guided my future, so talking to him sometimes seems optional.

What I discovered on those Wednesday nights in the upstairs classrooms at the end of a long hallway at Long Hollow Baptist Church was what I had been missing all these years. I discovered a God who wants to partner with us and invites us into an adventure with him but who also patiently waits for us to call down the resources of heaven and join him.

Jesus prayed continually and proactively, and heaven opened up because of it.

When Jesus prayed, the blind could see, the paralyzed walked, the mentally ill were given a sound mind, and even the sea became a path to walk on. Prayer was Jesus's principal language.

Jesus knew well what would happen to him. He knew he was

on earth to bring heaven and earth together for a few short years. He knew his mission was to sacrifice himself on the cross for our sins. He defeated death, hell, and the grave to make a way to eternal life for all who live for him.

He knew every second of his life, and he still prayed constantly. Why in the world had I lived so much of my life not talking to God daily?

For too long I viewed God's will for my life as static and done—my actions would ultimately have no effect on his will. If he wanted it, it would happen, and that was that. And my prayer life showed it.

During a season of study, I discovered a God who responds to our prayers and has even changed his mind because of his people's prayers. Moses was able to change God's mind when God was going to destroy the people of Israel because of their sin (Exodus 32). The Israelites were basically all of us, always doubting, forgetting, and complaining, and this time they really blew it. While Moses was spending time with God, the people melted all their gold and formed a cow to worship instead of worshiping God. God was ready to wipe them all out and start over, but Moses changed God's mind.

Yes, you read that right. The prayers of Moses changed the mind of God.

"I have seen these people," the LORD said to Moses, "and they are a stiff-necked people. Now leave me alone so that my anger may burn against them and that I may destroy them. Then I will make you into a great nation."

But Moses sought the favor of the LORD his God. "LORD," he said, "why should your anger burn against your people, whom you brought out of Egypt with great power and a mighty hand? Why should the Egyptians say, 'It was with evil intent that he brought them out, to kill them in the mountains and to wipe them off the face of the earth'? Turn from your fierce anger; relent and do not bring disaster on your people. Remember your servants Abraham, Isaac and Israel, to whom you swore by your own self: 'I will make your descendants as numerous as the stars in the sky and I will give your descendants all this land I promised them, and it will be their inheritance forever.'" Then the Lord relented and did not bring on his people the disaster he had threatened (Exodus 32:9–14).

God didn't change his mind because Moses knew better. God wasn't wrong and then saw the light. God is omniscient. He knows all. He changed his mind because he loved Moses and had compassion for people who deserved wrath.

God moves based on our prayers. Yes, prayer changes us, and that is important, but prayer actually changes things. God's character will never change, but he can and does change his mind based on our interactions with him. His mind will never be changed to something that is opposed to his plan for our lives, and we may never understand why some prayers are not answered the way we hoped they would be. But what I do know is **God is always listening, he cares about what we care about, and he moves on our behalf.**

Avoiding the Prayer Trap

Sometimes when God doesn't answer our prayers immediately, or he doesn't move in the way we prayed for, discouragement sets in.

Paul David Tripp writes,

Sadly, prayer for many of us has shrunk to an agenda that is little bigger than asking God for stuff. It has become a spiritual place where we ask God to sign our personal wish lists. For many, it is

little more than a repeated cycle of requesting, followed by waiting to see if God indeed comes through. If he does, we celebrate
his faithfulness and love; but if he doesn't, we not only wonder if
he cares, we are also tempted to wonder if he's there. In this way,
prayer often amounts to shopping at the Trinitarian department
store for what things you told yourself you need with the hope
that it will be free.[2]

**Real prayer is not just a list of requests or concerns. It's
a recognition that we are called to obey, created to worship,
and free to ask for what we need. Prayer is worship, surrender,
confession, and celebrating who God is and what he has done.**
Prayer can be a whisper of gratitude that the baby slept through
the night, a tearful confession when you realize you have strayed
from God, or a shared celebration with him that your prodigal has
come home. Prayer is fluid, never static, moving with you in every
season of life.

I'd love to tell you that through all God taught me, I had
learned to pray and then wait oh so patiently. But it was a process.
At first my prayers were rocket ships going up and asking for clarity. Then when I didn't get the answer I asked for, and on my time
table, I was mad. Then I was belligerent and told myself God had
a plan, his will would be done, and I couldn't do anything about it,
so I may as well quit praying about it.

I all but quit praying for a few months. I knew what God
wanted me to do, and I went along with his plan like a child reluctantly and somberly doing her most hated chores.

Leaving Blessings on the Table

There are possibilities God invites us to, but because we don't seek
him, ask him, and invite him into our daily lives, we miss out. We

leave power, help, resources, and blessing on the table because we forget we can ask for them.

This truth transformed how I lived.

God is not a God of lack. Yet somehow we live our lives believing he wants us to suffer.

It's as if we limp around this life forgetting he has just what we need.

We live our lives in weakness, forgetting that, as daughters of God, we have access to unlimited, unseen resources in him. We have the Holy Spirit in us giving us wisdom, strength, bravery, kindness, patience, and more.

The apostle Paul prayed:

For this reason I kneel before the Father, from whom every family in heaven and on earth derives its name. I pray that out of his glorious riches he may strengthen you with power through his Spirit in your inner being, so that Christ may dwell in your hearts through faith. And I pray that you, being rooted and established in love, may have power, together with all the Lord's holy people, to grasp how wide and long and high and deep is the love of Christ, and to know this love that surpasses knowledge—that you may be filled to the measure of all the fullness of God.

Now to him who is able to do immeasurably more than all we ask or imagine, according to his power that is at work within us, to him be glory in the church and in Christ Jesus throughout all generations, for ever and ever! Amen (Ephesians 3:14–21).

But how will God do "immeasurably more than all we ask or imagine"? How will he exceed our expectations if we don't have any? Just as I ask my coaching clients to wave their magic

> **TO STEP INTO THE LIFE GOD HAS CALLED YOU TO, YOU HAVE TO KNOW TRUTH AND PARTNER WITH IT.**

wands and share what life could look like for them over the next twelve months, I wonder what "immeasurably more" looks like to you. Get down on your knees and pray, just like the apostle Paul did. Instead of living in the land of "good enough," ask God to show you his "immeasurably more."

I had come this far in life learning to listen to him and learning to (sometimes reluctantly) obey him. Now it was time to learn to partner with him.

Called to Partner

Sometimes we think of the verse "The LORD will fight for you; you need only to be still" (Exodus 14:14) as an edict to *always* be passive, to shrug our shoulders and say, "If it's meant to be, God will do it." While it is true that God will accomplish his plan with or without us, he still calls us to do our part.

When you first looked into the eyes of your newborn and your heart swelled with hope for her future, your prayers were for her to be a great woman of God. Your dreams were for her to have a better life than you did, right? You didn't say, "Well, God's gonna do with you what God's gonna do. Good luck."

No way! You partnered with God to raise her right. You sacrificed and taught her what she needed to know. You armed her with wisdom. As she got older, you slowly taught her to do things herself so she could build strength for her journey ahead. You actively loved her every single day. You prayed for her; you fought for her. You and God partnered to raise this amazing woman of God.

We are called to work, called to partner, called to be active participants with God.

God determined my future, and my job was to roll up my sleeves and get to work. The work was mine to do, but God was the one who would breathe on it to succeed.

As I transitioned out of my role at work, I spent my weekends and evenings building the infrastructure and the plan to relaunch my coaching business. I knew that on April 1, I had to have a system to find new business coaching clients, systems to support those clients, and a million little action items all prepared and ready to go.

I couldn't say, "If it's God's will I leave this role and go it alone, I don't need to promote my work; he'll magically bring people to me."

I wish it worked like that. But sometimes we think it does, don't we? We think, "If it's meant to be, God will make it happen."

God asked Noah to build the ark, and Noah may have spent almost one hundred years making it happen. That man worked every day for decades, and you know there were so many people sitting on the sidelines telling him he was a fool, but he kept on working. He kept on working because he knew God was in it. (I found myself getting annoyed that rebuilding my business was taking longer than I wanted it to, and I was just a few months out.)

Maybe you've been there too. Maybe you have a dream of writing the next great novel and you are working on your writing skills and building your audience every day, but you secretly doubt it will ever happen because it's taking so long. Think of Noah swinging that hammer in years

> **GOD CALLS US TO WORK, TO MAKE THINGS HAPPEN, AND TO DO OUR PART HERE ON EARTH.**

twenty-six to thirty-five. Imagine his exhaustion. Year after year he worked. God could have made a perfect ark appear, but instead he called Noah to swing that hammer for decades.

God called Noah to be faithful to his calling, just like he calls us to keep showing up, every day, for as long as it takes.

Perhaps you feel called to start a business and you thought it would be easier than it has been. You secretly worry it's a sign you aren't in God's will because you come up against obstacle after obstacle. Imagine Noah cutting down trees, carrying them for miles, milling them, and climbing higher and higher to place them day after day and year after year. Imagine how he must have felt at year seventy-five.

I know how I would've felt. I'd be making my then middle-aged kids do the work, watching from my rocking chair and whispering in God's ear all day, "Am I crazy? Are you actually in this? I have lost my ever-loving mind!"

God partnered with Noah to build something new, just like he wants to partner with us.

Maybe God put it on your heart to pray for that lost person you love. And day after day, year after year, you pray and feel more worn down and disappointed that your prayers go unfulfilled. Imagine Noah at year ninety, wondering if his work was all a foolish waste of time.

God partnered with Noah to save his people, just like he partners with us to share the gospel and pray for those we love.

As a woman of God, you feel the call to create, to complement, and to complete. But living out that call, standing strong in the day-to-day, is always the challenge, isn't it? But each time we stand strong in our calling, we are getting in our reps, and God strengthens us. (Just think how strong Noah's arms were after swinging that hammer for decades!)

Sometimes we believe the lie that if we are meant to do something, God will wave his hand and magically it will be easy. But if we are going to partner with God, we have to know the truth, and the truth is, there is no easy button. **We wouldn't need to partner with God if we could do it on our own.**

If you are in a season of struggle, know that struggle is scriptural. All the great heroes of our faith struggled. That didn't mean they were doing anything wrong; it just meant life was hard . . . *is* hard, but here's the secret: with God we have unlimited, unseen resources on our side. God gives us wisdom, comfort, strength, and bravery in our hardest seasons, and all we need to do is ask him to help us.

I know that what you feel called to do is so much harder than you want it to be. I know because it's that way for every woman. Waking up every day and doing your job that makes your corner of the world a better place, investing in relationships that try your patience, building the dream that makes you feel like you are an elderly Noah sawing down trees in the desert, loving that neighbor who secretly makes you want to say things you'll have to ask Jesus to forgive you for later—these are difficult.

But you, great woman of God, created in his image to complete the whole of creation, are strong. You have been created with the same inherent strength that, when summoned, has the power to save nations (Esther), rescue armies (Joshua 2), bring healing (Luke 8:43–48), and give birth to a Savior (Luke 2:1–20). Not only that, but you are strong because the spirit of God lives in you. You are brave because an almighty, powerful God lives in you. You are worthy because you have been made worthy in Jesus.

Unfortunately, we live our lives as if these things aren't true, because we have never been taught to partner with truth. These words are a wake-up call that you don't have to live like you are on your own anymore.

Jesus tells us that he has come so we may have life and have it to the full (John 10:10). *He isn't talking about when we get to heaven; he means as soon as we become God's daughters.*

Living the Abundant Life

What does it look like for you to live life to the full? What do you want? What do you need? Spend some time thinking about it.

In my darkest season, afraid of not being able to provide for my family, I texted my friend Carol: "Carol, I'm scared. I only have a few more weeks working here and then that's it. The security of a steady paycheck is gone, and the weight of everything is back on my shoulders again." I didn't know how it would all come together.

She sent this text back to me:

> Alli, I know from my seat these are just faith questions, and from your seat these are, "Easy for you to say, Carol" questions. I understand that "your" time is running out. But God's isn't. I can't tell you what your future holds, and I can't tell you this won't be a rough season. But I don't doubt that God has a plan. Just keep moving forward until he shows you the plan. There is nothing more you can do. Ask him for manna. For strength to live off manna. Because after manna comes abundance. This is your testing ground to be a great woman of God.

Friend, I don't know what God has for you next, but I know the secret of how to find it. Complete the one action you feel confident he told you to do, spend time with him, pray like your life depends on it, and keep moving forward until he shows you the next step in the plan.

You Have Permission to Ask for What You Want

The Bible says, "You do not have because you do not ask God" (James 4:2).

Now I want you to start asking for what you need. Ask in full faith that the God who loves you, who sent Jesus to redeem you, will give you what is best for you. Often we don't know what is best for us. But you'd better believe the God who created the universe, who created you and loves you, sure does.

We don't have to put together beautiful and carefully crafted prayers. But we are told God hears us if we ask in accordance with his will (1 John 5:14). The problem is, we don't know God's will, so when we pour out our hearts to him in our own voices, from hearts and minds packed with our fears, we add on, "in accordance with your will, God." "According to your will" isn't meant to be our out in case he doesn't fulfill our wishes. We are meant to pray for God's will as a sign of humility that he knows best. The apostle John tells us, "This is the confidence we have in approaching God: that if we ask anything according to his will, he hears us. And if we know that he hears us—whatever we ask—we know that we have what we asked of him" (1 John 5:14–15).

We don't want him to answer our prayers that aren't best for us. If he did, I'd be married to that blond, Volkswagen Beetle–driving, skateboarding boy I loved in high school. I am forever relieved God didn't answer that prayer. I looked up that guy online, and to paraphrase Truvy in *Steel Magnolias*, the nicest thing I can say about him now is that all his tattoos are spelled correctly. God's future for us is better than we can imagine.

Sometimes God will answer our prayers if it is the best for us, sometimes we have to wait to get the answer, and sometimes he gives us something different that is aligned with his grand plan for our lives. But regardless, he wants us to ask because it places our hearts correctly in a place of dependence on him.

Jesus said to the blind man, "What do you want me to do for you?" (Mark 10:51). Imagine him asking you, "What do you want?"

Be brave and ask him. Ask him for wisdom, for strength, for power. Yes, I said power. The spirit of God lives in you, after all. Ask him to help you learn to access his power, to walk in it, and to grant you confidence and favor.

God wooed me into that theology classroom to show me I'm not alone, I'm not as weak as I feel, and he is here with unlimited resources. But I need to ask.

And likewise, God brought you here, right now in this moment, to tell you that you are not a victim of circumstances, you are not weak, you are not hopeless, and you are not alone.

Remember the words Carol gave me that day during my descent into desperation: "After manna comes abundance." No matter what you are going through right now, ask God for help, invite him in, and allow him to strengthen you. This is a step in your journey as a great woman of God.

Don't let yourself miss out on God's best for your life. Don't forget God is there for you. He is with you. He hears you. He loves you. He will never abandon you. And he is ready to partner with you to change you, change your life, and change your corner of the world.

I Want You to Remember

How we view God determines how we live our lives.

God's character will never change, but he can and does change his mind based on our interactions with him.

There are possibilities God invites us to, but because we don't seek him, ask him, and invite him into our daily lives, we miss out. We leave power, help, resources, and blessing on the table because we forget we can ask for them.

Instead of living in the land of "good enough," ask God to show you his "immeasurably more."

Discussion Questions

1. What we believe about God determines how we live our lives. How do your current beliefs about God dictate how you live?
2. Prayer was Jesus's principal language. He prayed continually and proactively. Is prayer your first response? If not, why?
3. What does it look like for you to live life to the full? What do you want? What do you need?

Action Steps

Prayer: James 4:2 says, "You do not have because you do not ask God." Ask God for what you need. Ask in full faith that the God who loves you, who sent Jesus to redeem you, will give you what is best for you. No matter what you are going through right now, ask God for help, invite him in, and allow him to strengthen you.

Journal: Read Ephesians 3:14–21. Give yourself permission to dream and answer this question: What does "immeasurably more" look like to me?

Practice: We are called to work, called to partner, called to be active participants with God. As you go to work, raise your family, volunteer, and so on, make it a habit to invite God into your work. Ask him for what you need, like innovation, creativity, strength, energy, resources, or favor with others.

Eleven

Get on the Other Side
of Obedience

I Want What God Has for Me

I did not die.

I did leave the job that meant security. I did leave the work I thought was so important. I did go back out on my own—on April Fool's Day, no less—and the world didn't collapse around me like my nightmares had predicted. The path ahead didn't seem any clearer than it had in those early days of hearing God tell me to leave my job, but I kept telling myself, "Clarity can wait. Obedience can't."

I accessed our savings account sooner than I hoped, ran up a little more credit card debt than I wanted, and ate way more almond milk ice cream than I should have, but little by little, coaching clients came. I started the marathon of rebuilding my business client by client, and now when I thought about taking care of my giant family, I finally felt like I could breathe again.

I hustled hard, and I took any and every shortcut that would save me time. Pajamas replaced business casual, showering daily was optional, and I decided cereal was the perfect time-saving lunch. I worked twelve-hour days six days a week. I told everyone I was back in business. I rebuilt my website, I launched ads, I sent emails to people on my email list, I reached out to old contacts—I did it all. Each day started with getting the kids off to school, then sitting down at my laptop and piece-by-painstaking-piece rebuilding my company. Here's what I didn't do: I didn't sit back and hope work would come to me. **I knew God was in the fight alongside me, but I also knew he wanted me to stand strong and show up for the battle.**

The easy part of all this was that I love coaching. I missed it those years I was away running the ministry. Coaching women—executives, business owners, entrepreneurs, leaders in all walks of life—is my sweet spot. I work with them on leadership, strategy, marketing, business expansion, and even helping with their lives and spiritual mentoring.

I say this not because I need the bragging rights but because it's the objective truth: I'm a great coach. (I had a hard time writing that sentence because women are culturally conditioned and rewarded not to be blunt or to own our gifts. So many of us are terrified at the thought of being seen as proud or full of ourselves, so we hide our gifts behind forced humility. But what if we lived in a world where, for women, saying, "I'm great at _____" was not only acceptable but encouraged? I want to live in that world, don't you? Let's make that world a reality together.)

Now sure, I have business expertise, but lots of people have that. And that's not even what makes me good at what I do. God somehow shows me what people need: what they need to do, what will work, and what won't. I can't even explain the process; somehow I always have the answers they need. It is how God gifted me, and I partner with him by leaning into the strengths he has given me.

But even with that gift, I was afraid. Would I be able to pay for the medicines and treatments that my son with migraines needed?

Would I be able to pay college tuition for all these boys? If Mark's asthma flared up, how would I manage it all?

These were the questions that woke me up at three in the morning and kept me company until the sun rose.

After years of uncertainty and struggle, I wanted a season of security, a season of rest. I didn't want life to be so uncertain all the time.

I didn't want to end up in a barn.

The Blessing of Obedience

Can I be too honest right now? I have helped clients build strategies and make millions in their businesses, yet I still sometimes lie in bed at night wondering if my business will fall apart.

You would think success and skill and even gifting would lead to security, wouldn't you?

They don't.

Obedience is the only path to security.

The problem with obedience is that it isn't sexy. No one wakes up in the morning saying, "Woo hoo! I'm pumped to obey God today." (Okay, if *you* do, you are way holier than I am.)

Obedience has been painted in the worst possible light. When we think of obedience, we either think of the way our kids obey (with attitudes and heavy sighs) or of some terrible boss we've had who insists on making our lives miserable (like Thomas the footman in the early years from *Downton Abbey*, who secretly sneers at Lord Grantham's commands).

Obedience seems like a "have to," not a "get to," type of scenario.

But for believers, obedience isn't the end of our freedom; it's the beginning of our blessing.

When we obey, we lose our ego and find our strength all at the same time.

Obedience is recognizing we follow the expert, the genius, the maker of the earth, who loves us, is on our side, fights for us, and knows exactly what we should do to live in abundance.

Disobedience clings to what feels safe and secure. But it's like drowning at sea because you won't let go of the mast of your sinking boat to grab hold of the ladder swinging from the rescue helicopter.

Disobedience leads to death because it is a lie that says you know better than God.

When you obey the Lord, he will bless you. This is because obedience always leads to blessing. That is a big statement, so let me tell you what I do and do not mean by the word *blessing*. I don't mean financial windfall. I don't mean we miraculously get rich or we receive payment in kind for our good behavior. Treating blessing like payment for good behavior reduces our lives in Christ to a religious sticker chart and his blessing to a token or a trinket. Blessing is so much more than that.

BEYOND OBEDIENCE IS YOUR BLESSING.

In the Gospels, Jesus asked Peter to put his boat into the water, just offshore, so Jesus could preach to the crowds that had gathered. It had been a long night of fishing, and Peter had little to show for it, but Peter obeyed, and he heard Jesus teach incredible parables. What a blessing (Luke 5:1–3).

When Jesus finished teaching the crowds, he told Peter to cast his nets into the water. Peter was tired. But once again, he obeyed, and his nets were filled to overflowing. What a blessing (Luke 5:4–7).

Peter was so overcome by God's blessing that he fell to his knees and worshipped Jesus immediately. Then Jesus commanded Peter (along with Andrew, James, and John), "Come, follow me . . . and

I will send you out to fish for people" (Matthew 4:19). Immediately they left their nets and followed him, becoming four of Jesus's twelve disciples. What a blessing.

> Every step of the way, Peter obeyed and blessing ensued.
> Noah obeyed and saved his family (Genesis 6:22). What a blessing.
> David obeyed and saved the Israelites (1 Samuel 17). What a blessing.
> Joseph obeyed and saved Egypt (Genesis 47:13–27). What a blessing.
> Abram obeyed and saved generations to come. (Genesis 12:1–8). What a blessing.
> Mary obeyed and gave birth to a savior (Luke 1:38). What a blessing.
> And then Jesus obeyed and saved the world (Matthew 26:36–42).

We have to get on the other side of obedience because blessing—life-changing, world-changing blessing—awaits.

God's blessing comes when we are all in. At the beginning of the book of Joshua, Moses has died and God is about to send the Israelites into the promised land. He's laying out some powerful promises to Joshua, their new leader. "I will give you every place where you set your foot. . . . No one will be able to stand against you all the days of your life. . . . I will never leave you nor forsake you" (Joshua 1:3, 5). All this blessing in exchange for a single posture: "Be strong and very courageous. Be careful to obey all the law my servant Moses gave you" (Joshua 1:7), which Moses himself did not obey, and we know how that turned out.

I love that God tells Joshua to "be strong and very coura-geous" before he tells him to obey. Sister, it takes serious courage to obey. If you want to see the promise of God and feel the power of God, you have to obey God's precepts. You have to do what he calls you to do.

What Is God Asking You to Do?

What is God asking you to do? Are you meant to leave your job and start a new season? Could you be called to mentor younger women? Maybe you feel God telling you to end a toxic relationship. Have you felt led to start a ministry that will help others heal? Is God telling you to confess an addiction to someone so you can get the help you need?

Be prepared, though, because when you choose obedience and take action, life often crumbles. Don't be surprised when your routines and rhythms grow more tumultuous for a season. **The enemy is going to throw everything he can at you to try to get you to slow down, to stop yielding to God, and to back away from God's promises and the future he has for you.**

I'm sure that when the Israelites stood on the banks of the Jordan River, they didn't think, "Cross a river at flood stage? No problem." I feel certain they thought, "We have to *cross a flooded river* to reach the promised land? Four hundred years in captivity weren't enough? Forty years wandering in the desert weren't enough? Now we have to cross a flooded river?"

And that wasn't all. They were commanded to circumcise all the males with a knife made from a sharpened rock once they made it to the other side. And then after that they were commanded to defeat a gigantic walled-off city by marching around it and blowing trumpets. That sounds terrible.

God called me to leave my job, and life got harder. When you obey God and walk into your calling, messiness often ensues.

Your kids who are normally well behaved will need more of
> your emotional energy.

You and your husband will have arguments about nothing.

You will receive an unexpected bill that makes you want to
> throw your hands up in defeat.

You will have moments when you feel like you made the
> wrong decision.

The enemy hates it when we walk in obedience, and he will
come in and whisper lies to your soul.

Some of his favorite lies are:

You thought you heard from God, but it was really you
> talking to yourself.

God may have come through every other time, but maybe
> this time he won't.

Who do you think you are? You can't do this.

I imagine the enemy was there whispering lies to Joshua and
the Israelites, taking advantage of the fact that their lives did not
get easier. But they obeyed anyway. And each step of the way, God
provided their needs and fulfilled his promises. They crossed the
river on dry land, he replaced manna with milk and honey, and he
gave them city after city after city.

Stand strong when the path grows thorny.

You may feel like you are weak and your obstacles are huge, but
don't believe the lie that you are a grasshopper and your problems
are giants. Your God controls it all, and you are important to him.

And don't be fooled into thinking all acts of obedience are huge
life-altering events.

Small acts of obedience require strength and courage too.

When God whispers to be kind to that woman whose kid

drives your kid crazy? That is obedience. When God reminds you to give to those in need? That's everyday obedience. When God softens your heart and nudges you to hug your husband after a fight? That's good, everyday, hard-to-do obedience.

Small day-to-day acts of obedience are what shape us into great women of God.

When God Speaks

I learned to trust and obey God even though I couldn't fathom all he had for me.

My only glimpse into my future was the word *preach*, which, if you ask me, always looks and sounds like so many different things.

I opened up my speaking calendar in faith, believing that when I was invited to come and speak at an event, I would have the physical ability to do so. I trusted that I would be able to get the words out and not whisper them between coughs.

I started my podcast with an overwhelming fear that I wouldn't be able to produce a weekly show because I didn't trust my voice to be there week to week. Each week while recording the podcast, I would record a little, take cough medicine, drink hot tea, and mute myself while my guests talked so I could cough and clear my throat. It was a mess.

He asked me to use my voice, so I obeyed. Even though I had no voice.

None of this made sense.

But I doubt marching around a city seven times while blowing trumpets made much sense either. Now, I'm not fighting the Lord's battle here, I know. But my life is the battle he has given me to fight. And your life is the battle he has given you to fight.

You fight every day when you choose love over hate, when

you bite your tongue instead of lashing out, and when you pull off the covers and tackle the day and all the problems that lie ahead instead of giving up and watching a season of *Gilmore Girls* while enjoying three bowls of Cinnamon Toast Crunch in your pink fluffy robe.

My job in that season was to fight. My fight was taking care of my health, taking care of my family, and taking care of my clients. I obeyed the command God had given me months before in the middle of the night: *Do what I taught you and fight.*

As the business grew strong and I paid off those credit card balances, I eased off the almond milk ice cream and wondered how in the world I'd bring those numbers on the scale back down.

On a sunny Wednesday morning, I sent the boys off to school and heard the wonderful pinging of my phone from across the kitchen. Somewhere, on some social platform, something was going down, and people were trying to get my attention. Whatever it was, I was there for it.

The pings were from Facebook. My Blissdom cofounder, Barbara, had shared a highlight video from one of our events, and the noise was hundreds of comments from attendees saying how much they'd missed Blissdom in the six years since it had ended.

Barbara texted, and we planned our next catch-up call. Ever since Blissdom had closed down, talking a couple of times a year had been our custom. No matter how much time passed, we remained good friends. I called her once and said, "I'm in New York City doing the *Today* show in the morning. I may die. I will probably throw up on camera. Need you to come and walk me through this." And being the legit friend she is, she took the train from Greenwich at five o'clock in the morning to reassure me I wouldn't die on live TV.

On our catch-up call we talked about our lives, our families, what all was going on, and she said, "Do you ever miss Blissdom?"

"Every single day I miss it."

"Do you ever think about having a Blissdom event again?"

"Absolutely not. I mean, I would love to, but God told me no. So no."

"Okay. Maybe just go think about it?"

I agreed, though I didn't give it much thought the rest of the day. And then the magic started happening.

I prayed.

Man, I wish I could hear God speak to me out loud. I would love an angel of the Lord to appear in my kitchen to tell me what's up. I'm here for that. I'd love a vision where I see clearly. I might think it was caused by bad leftover chicken, but I'd still love it. Yet such gifts never seem to materialize for me.

I hear a voice in my spirit that sometimes sounds an awful lot like my voice. Of course, I become confused and wonder, "Is this God or just wishful thinking on my part?" Sometimes I think, "Is God telling me to do this, or is the enemy saying this to distract me?"

I test what I hear to see if it's God, me, or the enemy. Untangling the person behind the voice is a lifelong job. It's like ordering food through a broken-down drive-through speaker. I hear something. And I'm pretty sure they are talking to me, but I'm so unsure of what is being said, I just sit there shaking my head.

Here's what I know to be true: God's voice and his commands match his character.

God speaks to us in a tone that is kinder and nicer than we would use to speak to ourselves.

The enemy speaks to us in a critical tone.

God never shames us. He will tell us when we are off course and bring us back with love.

The enemy speaks to us in a way that brings shame and self-loathing.

God will never ask us to do something that contradicts Scripture.

The enemy will tell us to sin and call it holy.

God's voice may ask you to accomplish tasks that are difficult and scary, but they will always be for your good and his glory.

The enemy will tell you to do things that will hurt you and those around you.

As I prayed about the idea of hosting the event again, I heard God whisper to my spirit, "*Yes*. It's time. You needed to grow, you needed to be humbled, and you needed to come back healthier. It's time."

Wow. I wasn't expecting that. Hosting Blissdom again would be a dream come true. Having permission to bring it back seemed too good to be true, and once again I wondered if I was hearing from God or Alli.

I needed confirmation. At this point, you know about my friend Carol, but here's the backstory of our friendship. About six years ago, God gave me the gift of my friend Carol. I met someone at a work function, and he went home to Houston and called his friend and said, "I met a woman, and I think you two should be friends." The craziest part is she actually called me, and we have been close friends ever since!

Continually, once or twice a year over the last six years, God gives Carol a message to give me that confirms or negates what I think he's been telling me. Just like when she confronted me that I had written a book on fear but was too afraid to obey God's call.

When I'm trying to sort through the voices in my head, sometimes I call Carol. Most of the time when I ask her to pray about something, she does, and she often tells me God has not spoken to her on my behalf. She speaks phrases such as, "It's not a crystal ball, Alli. God reveals what he chooses when he chooses." And sometimes she asks, "Did you ask him yourself?"

Knowing she would likely ask if I had talked with God myself, I prayed many times before I fired off this quick text to her:

> I've been talking to Barbara about the idea of hosting Blissdom again next year.

And?

> I think we are going to try to do it, but I need to run it by your discernment. 🙏🙏🙏

About six months ago, God told me you would host Blissdom again, but I was to say nothing. If I said something at that time, you would reject the idea and not think it was from him. But when you were ready to humble yourself, you'd attempt it, and you'd ask me what I thought. When you asked, I could then tell you what God said. I wrote in my journal.

> OMGosh. "When I humble myself." Really chewing on that. So it's ok?

Yeah. I don't know what "when you humble yourself" even means. But yes, yes, it's okay!

> Wow. I finally got a "yes." [I had been praying for so many business ideas God said no to that I forgot what a yes felt like.]

But Alli, I'd sure pray into that "Humble yourself" thing before you move ahead.

So there I was. I had my confirmation that God's telling me to host Blissdom wasn't really just me telling myself what I wanted to hear. (I've fallen into that trap more times than I'd like to admit.)

I called Barbara and announced, "God's in it. Book the venue. Blissdom is back!"

Never did I even entertain the idea that Blissdom could come back. God had me walk away. It was done. He would never have me hold a business conference again. I thought when God wrote a conclusion, the story was over, done, finished.

God is a God of restoration and restarts. He was resurrecting something I sacrificed long ago. Something I never even knew I could pray for the redemption of. Something I thought was long dead.

I don't know what it is that feels dead in your own life, but I know God is a God of miracles, second chances, and new beginnings.

Is there something in your life that you feel is dead? Something beyond the ability to be resurrected? Maybe your bags are packed and you're ready to walk out on your dead, lifeless marriage. Maybe your child's addiction has severed their relationship with you and there's no finding your way back this time. Maybe the demands of your busy life have suffocated your dreams so long they'll never breathe again.

WHO ARE WE TO SAY WHAT IS DEAD WHEN WE SERVE A GOD WHO BRINGS THE DEAD BACK TO LIFE?

I want to remind you that God is "able to do immeasurably more than all we ask or imagine according to his power that is at work within us" (Ephesians 3:20). That includes resurrecting what we have long since counted as dead.

God could have told me two years before, "Alli, quit your job, rebuild your business, speak and use your voice for me, and guess what, girl? Just for fun, I'm bringing Blissdom back." He could have. He knew the whole time. He knew before I was born what would happen. He knew what would happen before he even created the world.

God had other plans for me, as he does for us all.

He doesn't give us all the answers or a crystal ball to see the future. Instead, he strengthens our relationship with him by giving us opportunity after opportunity to trust and be trusted.

He invites us into a partnership.

He gives us hope and causes us to believe in what we'd long since considered dead.

He is better than you think. The future he has for you is better than you think. And the biggest shocker of all is, obedience will be better than you think.

If you want to see the power of God in your life, if you want to see his promises fulfilled, if you want to access the unlimited, unseen resources of the Lord Most High, get on the other side of obedience, walk in your calling, and bask in his blessing—the most ultimate blessing being the presence of God with you wherever you go.

I Want You to Remember

For believers, obedience isn't the end of our freedom; it's the beginning of our blessing.

Disobedience clings to what feels safe and secure. Disobedience leads to death because it is a lie that says you know better than God.

When you choose obedience, the enemy is going to throw everything he can at you to try to get you to slow down, to stop yielding to God, and to back away from God's promises and the future he has for you.

God doesn't give us all the answers or a crystal ball to see the future. Instead, he strengthens our relationship with him by giving us opportunity after opportunity to trust and be trusted.

Discussion Questions

1. Clarity can wait. Obedience can't. Are you currently waiting on clarity to take the step of obedience?
2. Blessing is on the other side of obedience. What steps do you need to take to get on the other side of obedience?
3. God is able to do immeasurably more than all we ask or imagine according to his power that is at work within us. What are you currently imagining?

Action Steps

Prayer: Next time you're prompted to ask God, "Help me to understand," say instead, "Help me to obey."

Journal: With your journal in hand, ask God, "What does obedience look like for me in this season?" Write down what you sense him saying. Read through what you wrote, and identify the next step you need to take to walk in obedience. Make sure this next step is actionable. For example, writing a book may be your goal, but finishing a first draft of your book proposal would be an actionable next step.

Practice: Share your next step with a trusted friend. Ask them to partner with you in prayer and by checking in with you to keep you accountable. Take the next step!

Twelve

Do It Scared

I'm Willing to Take the First Step

Standing there in front of my mirror, my towel haphazardly wrapped around my freshly washed self, I pulled my wet hair back in a bun. In the foggy mirror, something different caught my eye. I know my face's details: the dark circles under my eyes from staying up too late talking to a teenage son about life and the crow's-feet that crawl across my face, deeper each year. I comfort myself with, "It's from so much laughter."

Some days I see my reflection and feel like I don't know who is looking back at me. I still feel like I'm twenty-five, but I'm caught in the body of a much older woman. And my vanity whines to stop the march of time across my face and slow the spread of my backside that seems to have a mind of its own. "I guess I have to admit I'm a grown up now," I mumble with a resigned laugh, no matter how I feel inside.

Most of the time, I've made peace with aging. I like who I am in my forties. I've fought long and hard to feel comfortable in my skin. With culture's nonsense thrown at us every day that we have to look a certain way and be the right size and shape, my battles to accept the body God gave me are hard won and have to be refought often.

But what was different about me today?

The past five years had given me some extra pounds, wrinkles that popped up in new places, and, to make matters worse, hair loss. The hair loss started a few months after God told me to leave my job, but my hair kept on thinning. My hair and I were friends, so I was pretty disappointed at its betrayal, its decision to leave me after so many great years together. Did I need more vitamins? Added hormones? Better conditioner? Less highlighting?

It had never occurred to me that stress was the culprit.

I had spent months frozen in fear, paralyzed by what-ifs, and focused on my shortcomings. I rode that wave of panic like a toddler on a Slip 'N Slide. And the stress of it all had taken its toll.

But that day, in my towel in front of my mirror, fussing over my latest wrinkles, I saw something new. I saw hope. With my hair wet and pulled back, I saw a new layer of hair beginning to grow back.

If you've had a baby, you know what I'm talking about. One day you have a gorgeous mane of hair fueled by hormones and pregnancy vitamins, and then childbirth, sleepless nights, breastfeeding, and different hormones cause your hair to fall out. The hair loss happens slowly at first and then escalates until you wonder if it will ever end. The loss of your hair feels like one more way your body, along with everything else in the universe, is betraying you.

Then it happens. You notice those baby hairs growing back in around your face, and you take in the first deep breath you've had in a long time. That new hair is your body's way of saying, "I've got you girl. We're gonna be okay."

That new hair was my sign of hope.

It wasn't that my fear was magically gone and my hair came back. I didn't wake up every day with confidence and feel like I was killing it all of a sudden. I still wrestled with anxiety and took shaky steps of faith.

I guess my body decided I was going in the right direction. I was still scared as I moved into the next season, but I was moving. Step-by-step, I was taking action, breaking out of the prison of fear that kept me locked up for too long.

Confidence Comes from Taking Action

My body slowly began to heal.

My hair grew back, my round-the-clock stomach and chest pain subsided, and that cough—my constant companion—slowly disappeared. It was if my body gave me its blessing to keep doing it scared. I was out of my comfort zone, but I was moving toward God.

New rhythms and different routines can sometimes cause fear or anxiety in our lives. When we learn a new baby is on its way, we worry whether we will be good parents. When a new promotion or career opportunity comes, we fear we aren't up to the task. When we imagine stepping with even just one toe out of our comfort zone, we become anxious.

Our comfort zone is where we believe we will be cared for, where we know we can do a great job, and where life is safe and secure. It's where we can live life cuddling in a fuzzy blanket, eating snacks, and never worrying about tomorrow.

But God's call to more is a call to abandon what creates comfort. Everything of meaning, of wonder, of beauty, and of happiness happens outside where we feel comfortable.

Your baby makes you uncomfortable in every way possible—from the swollen ankles to the sleepless nights rocking your little nine-pound dictator back to sleep. Your dream of starting a business to help so many people will require pain, sacrifice, and stepping out past your fear. Your call to write a book will force you to wrestle with your own insecurity and make you decide whether you believe the voice of God who calls you more than the voice of self-doubt. Your dedication to restore your marriage will require self-control, empathy, and more grace than you ever knew you had.

When we live outside our comfort zones, we hold on to the comfort of God and these truths he offers:

Our fear makes us insecure. Our God makes us confident.

Our fear tells us we can't. Our God tells us he is able.

Our fear says we'll fail. Our God says he's already won.

Our fear tells us to freeze. Our God tells us to fly.

We can feel afraid and do it anyway because God is the one calling us to the unknown.

Feeling fear and doing it anyway is the difference between staying frozen in fear and living a life of meaning and purpose.

Launching Out of Overwhelm

Every morning when I opened my eyes, I felt a new wave of overwhelm. Building my business back up was working, and I was making ends meet, but waves of anxiety still washed over me. Having a full slate of clients, hosting my weekly show, being a wife and mom and person who showers occasionally—it all felt overwhelming.

I fell into an old trap that I knew all too well. You may have gotten your foot caught in it a time or two yourself. It's the trap of self-sufficiency. I behaved like I believed God was busy. With a little nod of appreciation to God for all his help, little by little I took control. When life felt off course, I tried harder. When my anxiety nudged up a bit, I worked more.

God had set my feet on the right course, and I was going to show him that I could do it.

Alone.

Once again, I was that toddler on the Slip 'N Slide, careening forward at a breakneck pace, destined to crash but unable to stop myself.

It was like when my oldest son, Justin, was learning to walk. He was so stubborn about doing it himself. He let me help him up when he fell, but once he was standing, he wanted to go it alone. He'd take a few awkward steps, then the weight of his body would throw him forward. It never took long for him to stumble and eventually wipe out completely. Mark helped Justin see that if he'd just hold on to one of his dad's hands, he could still walk on his own. He didn't have to be carried for the rest of his life, but he didn't have to go it alone either.

So many times I feel like I am like my child learning to walk. I want to do it alone, but it doesn't have to be that way. I don't have to live life in my own power. None of us do.

When we try to live life in our own power, pulling ourselves up by the proverbial bootstraps, it's a recipe for overwhelm, self-doubt, and burnout.

God is there, waiting to partner with us. Taking his hand doesn't mean we're asking to be carried for the rest of our lives. It means we're slipping control into the comfort of the hands that carry the world. We partner with God when we invite him into every part of our lives and continually remind ourselves that our strength, our wisdom, our power, and our courage are from him.

There were still many mornings I wanted to let fear get the best of me. Many mornings I wanted to pull the covers back over my head because it all felt overwhelming. But I would whisper, "God did not give me a spirit of fear, but power, love, and self-control. Five, four, three, two, one, go!" And I'd launch myself out of bed.

Remember the five-second secret? I knew my brain was going

to try to trick me into protecting myself from anything that felt uncomfortable. But I was partnering with God. As silly as I felt counting down, if I had to trick my brain to take action, then so be it.

I also started holding up my hand to God like a child reaching up for the comfort of his parent as he learns to walk. Each time I started feeling like I was behind with my work and wanted to go binge-watch episodes of *The Crown* to avoid my responsibilities, I'd stick my hand up in the air, like Wonder Woman about to go beat up some bad guys, and I'd say, "God didn't give me a spirit of fear but of power and love and self-control. Five, four, three, two, one, go!" And I would tackle my to-do list like a woman on a mission.

After a year of letting fear stop me, I had learned the secret to doing it scared.

I had wanted to know in advance what God's provision would be. I wanted to know that all the bills would be paid and I wouldn't fail to take care of my kids. I wanted to make sure that my act of wild faith wasn't my being an irresponsible or selfish mother. I wanted to know I could take care of Mark if the bottom fell out on his health again. I wanted to know every last detail of when, what, and exactly how God would arrange my life.

But God knew better. God knew that the process of my listening, trusting, and obeying would build something in me that wouldn't grow if I knew the answers in advance.

Sometimes it takes walking through seasons of heartache, loss, fear, or uncertainty to build the strength, resiliency, and power that he has for us. He allows us to walk. He allows us to fall. But he doesn't expect us to do it without him.

What does fear look like in your life? What do you dream of doing yet still resist? What do you talk yourself out of?

Sometimes we play small because we see the gap between where we are now and where God is leading us, and the chasm seems so wide that you believe it can't be crossed.

I recently heard a story about a woman named Annie, who at thirty-two years old decided she wanted to learn to drive a car. As a sixteen-year-old, she wrecked her dad's car while learning to drive, and she had never driven a day again in her life. A wife, a mother of two, and an accomplished accountant with her own business, she couldn't drive a car.

It was a constant source of embarrassment to her, but her fear had been the driver for so long, she couldn't see ever getting out of the passenger's seat.

When her nephew moved out to the country, he convinced her to learn to drive out on his rural property. She was terrified, but each time she got behind the wheel of the car, she felt a little more confident. She moved from driving on the farm to driving down the country road to eventually driving herself home.

When she pulled in the driveway, she laid on the horn. Her family saw her behind the wheel, and they all came running out the door, screaming and celebrating with her. She kicked fear to the back seat, and although fear sometimes still wanted to drive, she never let it take the wheel again. Annie said goodbye to playing small once and for all.

How to Move Forward When Fear Holds You Back

Fear screams at us when we are on the cusp of a new season ripe with strength and beauty. It is the biggest hindrance to our living up to our potential and overcoming what holds us back. And the only way to face it and move forward is to roar back with truth, even if we have to start small and scary.

YOU CAN DO ANYTHING IF YOU ARE WILLING TO MOVE FORWARD AND MAKE A SMALL AND SCARY START.

In this scariest of seasons, worn down by some hard years, with a few extra pounds from stress eating and a few more wrinkles from worry but armed with a head full of new hair growing back, I asked myself a simple question.

In my situation right now, what would a great woman of God do?

As I thought about Annie, I developed four steps to keep me moving forward.

1. Step Back and Gain Perspective

When we seek to do anything in our lives—write a book, teach the Bible, go back to school, get in shape, learn to drive a car—everything in us says, "Nah. I'm good," as if it were a great idea but not worth the effort.

When we step back and gain some perspective, we are able to say, "I can do this. It is worth it. I just have to put my hands on the wheel, give it a little gas, and go. I don't have to go far; I just have to go forward."

2. Pray for Strength and Courage

When we ask God to make our paths clear, when we ask for strength and courage to do the next right thing, he walks with us.

I feel certain that when Annie got behind the wheel of that car for the first time, she was praying. I know she prayed for strength and for courage and to remember which pedal was the brake and which was the accelerator. She probably had a prayer list as long as the drive from the country to her house. She needed God like she'd never needed him before, and there was no way she was driving that car without him sitting right next to her in the passenger seat.

God is as excited about partnering with us as we are about moving forward. We like to think maybe our prayer is all old news to him, but he is overjoyed when we pray. He's like Annie's family coming out the door when she honked. He is all in.

3. Act with Intention and Take One Step

We can gain perspective and pray for strength, but we have to take action.

Being still and waiting on the Lord doesn't mean sitting around waiting for the grass to grow. You have to take the next step and put your faith into action. Yes, God's timing is important. God is usually the one waiting on us. He's waiting on us to trust, waiting on us to obey, and waiting on us to move. But you have to get going, act with intention, and take one step.

Imagine what would have happened if the Israelites hadn't taken that first step into the Red Sea (Exodus 14:13–30). Think about Peter's faith and what he would have missed out on had he not stepped out of the boat (Matthew 14:22–33). Picture the story of the paralytic's four friends. What if they had never dug through the roof to get to Jesus (Mark 2:1–12)? What about the woman who reached out to touch the hem of Jesus's robe (Mark 5:25–34)?

Every single one of these people took one scary intentional step. And you can too.

Start by saying one prayer.

Do one lap around the track.

Read one chapter in the Bible.

Say you're sorry to one person.

Make one sale.

Write one paragraph.

Send one text.

Just like Annie, we have to make the decision to start the car before we can move forward.

4. Look for How to Serve

When I am wrapped up in myself, serving others is what unwraps me. It takes my mind off me and also motivates me to become the great woman of God I was created to be. God created me to partner with him to make a difference in the world. We aren't going on a joyride here. We have a purpose.

Annie was motivated by the knowledge that she would ease her husband's and friends' burdens by learning to drive. They wouldn't have to continually stop their lives to transport her. The thought of serving them drove her (pun intended) to conquer her fears.

Your Kingdom Work

I don't know what mountain is in front of you. I don't know what God has placed in your heart. I don't know what lies the enemy whispers to your soul to block you from walking into your destiny. But I do know you are reading my story for a reason. *God placed us in each other's paths by grand design.* My story, your story—they are the same story as those of millions of other women. Same story. Different details.

God calls, we are sure it will all fall apart, we can't imagine that we are up for what he is calling us to, we take shaky steps in obedience, and he shows up.

Every single time.

Knowing this truth, I'm kind of embarrassed to admit that even though God has walked me through dark nights and seasons of wavering faith, even though he has waited patiently for me to trust him enough to obey, doubts still occasionally go through my mind in the middle of the night.

What if this is the time he doesn't show up?

What if his will is for me to fail for some reason?

What if this isn't his plan, and I really am alone?

The moment before we take action and do it scared is always filled with what-ifs, worst-case scenarios, and visions of disaster.

The enemy will come and whisper lies just like he has been doing since the garden of Eden. He knows your vulnerabilities. He is smart, and we have to be smarter.

Your work matters. Whether you are teaching in a classroom or teaching your kids not to put beans up their noses. Whether you are filing legal briefs or washing your briefs. Whether you are counseling clients or counseling a friend across coffee. *It's kingdom work and it matters to God.*

Whatever your kingdom work is, it is holy, set apart by God, and important. The enemy will take notice and try to take you out. He wants to distract you, depress you, and discourage you. The attacks, the struggle, and the fear are a normal part of getting where you are going.

Your fear is not a sign you aren't meant to move forward. Feel the fear and do it anyway. Soon the fear will back down.

Just like God gave me hope through baby hairs that morning in front of my mirror, he'll give you hope with each baby step you take.

Baby step it into your destiny, sister. Your calling is worth it. You are worth it. And eventually those scared baby steps will become easier and you'll be well on your way to feeling like the great woman of God you already are.

I Want You to Remember

Feeling the fear and doing it anyway is the difference between staying frozen in fear and living a life of meaning and purpose.

When we try to live life in our own power, pulling ourselves up by the proverbial bootstraps, it's a recipe for overwhelm, self-doubt, and burnout.

You can do anything if you are willing to move forward and make a small and scary start.

Your work matters. Big or small, it's kingdom work and it matters to God.

Discussion Questions

1. Confidence comes from taking action. What actions can you take today to build your confidence?
2. What things do you dream of doing that you hold yourself back from? What are you currently talking yourself out of doing?
3. In your situation right now, what would a great woman of God do?

Action Steps

Prayer: Develop a habit of seeking comfort from God amid uncomfortable circumstances. When you find yourself lacking peace or comfort, take that feeling to God in prayer. Ask him for the strength and courage to do the next right thing.

Journal: God has created you to partner with him to make a difference in the world. Who will be served by your living out your calling? Write about this group of people. If you don't know who specifically will be served, ask God for clarity on the types of people who will be served (think attributes, demographics, geographic locations). Then ask yourself, "Are these people worth my conquering my fear and moving forward on their behalf?"

Practice: It's time to take action. What is the next step toward your dream? Don't think of the big long list of steps it will take you to reach that dream. (Though it's fine to make the list if that helps you.) Think of the first scary step, and do that one thing.

Thirteen

Trust the Process

I Choose to Believe

"I can see it for her, Mark, so why am I so full of doubt for myself?" The question was more rhetorical than anything else, but Mark punched up his pillow, then rolled over and looked at me, searching my face to see if I planned to continue.

I thought about the situation with Jessica, one of my coaching clients.

Jessica worked for a great company, had great benefits, and was in a position people work their entire careers to reach. But she knew she couldn't stay. God had asked her to step out in faith, to leave her career-defining job and forge out into the unknown with him. Dragging her feet to leave was sucking her soul daily, a feeling that was all too familiar to me. I was great at telling her what to do. It was so clear to me, and I couldn't understand why she wasn't taking that step of obedience.

And then she did it. At my encouragement, she made the decision to leave, despite all the fear she faced. But I never would have guessed that after two months of job searching, she'd still be looking.

On paper, she had everything: she was a mover and shaker in her industry, her list of achievements was a mile long, she was well respected, and she brought her kingdom heart to the corporate world.

"Jessica, God has never let you down, has he? He's not about to start now. You have a history with him. Look back over the timeline of your partnership together. You can see every place where he has moved, provided, and been faithful to keep his promises. You have to be faithful too." It seemed like that was my ongoing coaching with Jessica for months.

Despite what was happening to Jessica, I never doubted God, and I wouldn't let Jessica doubt him either. "Jessica, you can't see it, but God is teaching you to stand strong in a way that is so powerful it will carry you through many hard seasons to come. He is shaping you into the great woman of God you are meant to be."

Even as I spoke the words to her, I knew I didn't believe them for myself. Thus, my pillow-talk confession to Mark.

It wasn't long before Jessica was in the perfect role, one that only God could have orchestrated, in which she worked from home several days a week, directing and leading company culture. It far exceeded her hopes and dreams.

I never doubted God's plan for her. Not once. But in the midst of encouraging Jessica, I spent a mountain of days begging God to keep helping me. I had no trouble seeing his plan for Jessica, but I doubted God's plan for *me*.

Isn't that comical—and isn't that common? Sometimes we see so clearly for others. We give the best advice, pray the best prayers, and walk in the strongest, fiercest faith—for them. But for ourselves, all we see is the storm. All we hear is the sound of the wind in our ears. All we believe is what the waves crashing over the bow tell us.

When we watch others' situations, we're often able to keep our eyes on the Lord. We see their storm, but we see God through it. We hear the wind, but we hear God through it. We see the waves, but we aren't afraid of capsizing. The enemy isn't distracting us, because it's not our life he's trying to derail.

Of course I could be strong for Jessica. I wasn't weathering her storm.

In my own storm, being strong wasn't as easy, even though God was strengthening me just like he was Jessica. And just like Jessica, though I still doubted, I took those scary steps of obedience.

I know there are many of us who have had to trust God in the process. Like Jessica, many of us have had to walk through the same transition of working from home. Only, in your story, it might not have been something you wanted. It might not have been something you prayed for or planned for. Working from home, for many women who might be reading this right now, might be the result of the global pandemic that has touched all our lives.

You too have had to trust God in the process. You've had to trust him in the homeschooling and in the job losing as you watched the world wage war with an invisible enemy—the violent virus that wreaked havoc in all our lives.

Could it be that even through the pandemic, our God has called us into partnership and not passivity? Could it be that, even through some of the deepest and widest pain we've ever known, our God has drawn us closer to his heart—and our callings?

Partnership, Not Passivity

My cousin Leanne loves to cook popcorn the old-fashioned way—in a pan, with hot oil. She pours the oil into the pan, turns up the heat, drops in the kernels, puts on the glass lid, and waits.

Gradually the oil heats up, and the kernels start to bubble in the hot oil. Through the glass lid we watch, waiting for the moment when the insides of the kernels reach such an intense heat that they explode out of their shells. When they explode, I'm always reminded that big things arise from small beginnings if we wait.

Watching Leanne's kids wait for the kernels to pop reminds me of my impatience. To them, the kernels always seem to take forever to heat up. Waiting for them to burst is excruciating. But the kids' process of waiting is filled with excitement because they know what's coming.

Just as those kernels grow, expand, and transform after heat and pressure are applied, we ourselves transform through times of struggle.

Our times of pressure, heat, and struggle will bring out our best.

> **OUR TIMES OF PRESSURE, HEAT, AND STRUGGLE WILL BRING OUT OUR BEST.**

Waiting is where the best stuff happens. Blessings come from seasons of waiting. All throughout the Bible we see that believing, hoping, and waiting go hand in hand. (Many Bible scholars use the words *hope* and *wait* interchangeably.) We know from Scripture that waiting leads to strength.

> They who wait for the LORD shall renew their strength;
>> they shall mount up with wings like eagles;
> they shall run and not be weary;
>> they shall walk and not faint. (Isaiah 40:31 ESV)

The Hebrew word used for "wait" in this verse is *qavah*.

Qavah means "to wait, hope for, look, expect," and it also means "to gather."[1]

Here's the thing about this passage of Scripture: it is quoted so often that its impact has been reduced to a nice font on a cool graphic. But it's so much more than that. Read Isaiah 40:31 again.

Feel the expectancy for the Lord to act. You can almost feel the strength gathering up inside. *Qavah* is the same word the Lord used in relation to the Israelites waiting to be freed from captivity in Babylon.[2] This is an active, deeply earnest, faith-filled waiting, hoping, and looking forward to how God will move. This *qavah* is partnership. We join him expectantly.

Waiting on God for breakthrough helps us learn how to trust the process. Where we go wrong is when we think we are meant to wait passively instead of having a partnership mentality. Waiting on the Lord isn't like waiting in a carpool line or being stuck in the purgatory that is the DMV line. We aren't meant to just suffer through and distract ourselves until our time comes.

Waiting, for us as women of God, is a time when we lean in and cultivate a spirit of expectancy. We pray for, and thank God in advance for, the answers to our prayers, the breakthroughs we wait for, the clarity we seek.

Waiting doesn't mean allowing ourselves to be paralyzed with fear and doubt; it means moving forward (yes, even in those single, scared, shaking steps) in courage to build our strength. Waiting means we allow God to do the heavy lifting, the deep heart-change work inside us while we keep powering through.

Waiting on him to step in and move doesn't mean we sit idly by and say, "I'll simply wait for the Lord to fight for me." God steps in and relocates mountains on our behalf, but we forget he still expects us to keep working in the meantime.

God gave me the skills to earn the money to buy my cereal, but he expects me to go to work, deposit my check, go to the store, pour the bowl, and feed myself.

God trusts us too much to do everything for us without our involvement. He partners with us to strengthen us.

GOD WON'T DO FOR YOU THE TASKS HE HAS GIVEN YOU TO DO.

He expects us to work hard and get strong.

It's a lot like how we don't baby our kids when we are teaching them to be self-sufficient, to stand strong on their own two legs. We give them situations to grow into; they have to stretch, figure it out for themselves, walk on wobbly legs, fall down a few thousand times, build their strength, and walk.

Same with us, sister. Waiting on the Lord looks like partnering with him so we can do his work on earth. And we wait expectantly while we do our part. While we do our work, we wobble, fall, and build our strength.

And just like a toddler doesn't fall a few times and decide, "I guess I'm not cut out for walking. I'm just going to plop down and wait for my parents to carry me through life," we can't live like that is an option either. We can't plop down and wait for God to carry us through life.

But we do it all the time, don't we? We sit down in defeat when we fall. We play small when self-doubt washes over us. We take ourselves out of the game before we ever get a chance to play.

And we call it holy. We call it good. We call it "waiting on the Lord."

Ain't nothin' holy about giving up when God calls you to get strong.

Our seasons of waiting and actively partnering with God change us. We learn how to trust him, how to stop demanding our own way, how to humble ourselves and yield to his plan, how to praise him before his promise is fulfilled, and how to prepare for the future he planned for us.

For me, months of waiting for God to come through looked like normal life—working, being a chauffeur to my kids, going to sports practices and youth groups, making dinner, and living life in the day-to-day. Life went on, but I knew deep in my heart that I was still struggling.

And just like God has done so many other times in my life, he reached me through music.

I love worship music. It wrecks me in all the best ways. When I was writing *Fierce Faith*, I created an online eighteen-hour worship playlist called Worship for Fierce Faith.[3] These songs have become an anthem for me and for thousands of women. They remind us of God's faithfulness even when our hearts waver.

In my most hard-hearted seasons, God has always reached me with music. It has been my comfort, my connection to him, my declaration, and my prayer when I can't find my words.

During my illness, my daily routines shifted. Even my eating habits changed, sadly. I love junk food. But my stomach turned against me, and I had to learn to eat foods without dairy and wheat. I learned the hard way why Whole Foods is called "whole pay-check." One sunny day I was walking out of Whole Foods feeling sorry for myself because I wanted all the chocolate but didn't buy all the chocolate, and my friend Steph texted and said, "You need to listen to this one right now." She linked to the song "Do It Again" from Elevation Worship.

The words of that song tell of seeing God move mountains over and over again. It's a song that reminds us to believe God can and will make a way, even when we can't see it.

I sat there in my car and sang a declaration over my life. I sang to convince myself that God wasn't going to let me down this time or anytime. He had never failed me yet.

"Do It Again" became my anthem in the waiting season. I listened to it so much that the boys would say, "Mom, what is up with this song? Do we have to hear it again?"

I sang it over my life like honey on a hot biscuit. It was my comfort, my declaration that even though I was weak, God was strong; even though I was fallible, he was not; even though nothing looked right, he was making a way.

We all have soundtracks in our lives: the words we say to ourselves, the inner critic we have to learn to tame, the voices we listen to, the music we listen to. My soundtrack, as I learned to trust God's timing and his process, was a steady flow of worship music.

I sang that God was the "King of My Heart" and he was never, ever, ever going to let me down. *You've brought me this far, God, and never let me down before, and I'm not going to let the enemy tell me otherwise.*

I sang with "Great Are You Lord" that God alone was great and I worshipped him alone. *One day my voice will return, my lungs that you created will clear, and I will sing your praise out loud with a real voice again no matter how impossible it feels.*

I sang that his "Reckless Love" was for me and he was chasing me down. *You won't let me go. You marked me. You fought for me. You are good to me. You are coming after me. I'm not left on my own.*

I sang with "New Wine" that I yielded to his careful hand and trusted him even when I didn't understand. *I don't need to know your plans; it's my job to partner with you, to submit to your plans for me and to let you make me whatever you want me to be.*

The waiting, the in-between, the messy middle is where the good and the hard stuff is. Welcome to your divine middle ground. This is where your wobbly legs get strong, where the voice you've lost comes back. It's where the heart that was broken gets healed.

We learn to partner with him in the messy middle.

We partner, and we take action, step by scary step.

We partner, and we do our work.

We partner, and we learn new skills.

We partner, and we face our fears.

We partner, and we pray for breakthrough.

We partner, and we thank him in advance for rescue.

We partner, and we worship even through our doubts.

We partner, and we proclaim his faithfulness.

When we trust his timing and the process he has us in, it's a game changer.

Instead of letting fear, self-doubt, and heartache sideline us, we get back in the game.

We grow strong, we let the trials build our character, and we become light to the world.

As I write the resolution of my season of waiting, I find myself in a new waiting game.

Today, as I write the end of my last story, I'm also in the messy middle of a new story, a story full of partnering with God, praying for healing, and thanking him in advance for the healing that we believe will come. This new story I'm living is a story of waiting, trusting the process and God's timing, believing his ways are greater than ours, and declaring that all will come together for our good.

One of my sons has debilitating migraines that have put his life on hold. We have seen all the doctors, tried all the medications, and still he suffers in extreme pain daily. There's no sorrow like that of a mother who has to watch her child suffer. Some days I'm hopeful, some days I'm angry, and some days I'm confused about why it's taking so long to help him.

It's as though I'm standing on the mountaintop and seeing the valley, all while standing in the valley and seeing the mountaintop.

I might have nothing but messy middles in plain sight, but I am surrounded by his majesty, his miracles, and his might.

Our lives are lived in the valleys and the mountaintops, the pain and the promise, the heartache and the rescue. **We are always living in the tension of the now and the not yet.** And we yearn for the not yet that is to come.

None of us have the secret to living a pain-free Christian life. We can only learn to yield to the One who holds our lives in his hands. We can only trust his goodness and stand strong in him on the mountaintops of victory and in the valleys that feel like hell.

My life and your life—they aren't going to get any easier, but God is going to make us stronger. I'm here to talk straight to you. I'm not your hype girl; I'm your "let's get strong" girl. Let's learn to be women who bear that burden well, who carry the weight he gives us with strength, and do it all for our good and his glory.

We are all on timelines that only our Maker knows. You are on the timeline that God has for you. God has put a unique and perfect mix of gifts in you. He trusts you with those gifts. And he is building strength in you to bring them to the world in new ways.

There are gifts inside you that have been there your whole life, gifts you uncover with every year that unfolds. They are entrusted to you. The more you develop them in your season of waiting, the more he can use them in the future.

You may be thinking, "I know what my gifts are, but I'm so frustrated that I can't use them. I know I'm called, but all the doors keep closing in front of me. I just need a chance. I need a chance to use what God has given me."

I hear you. I understand. I can't pretend I know the answers, but I can remind you of who does.

Soul Tending

David was in just as much shock as his father and brothers when the prophet Samuel anointed him as the future king of Israel. He'd been busy tending sheep when his father called for him. And somehow, out of Jesse's eight sons, he was the one God chose.

What was David to do now? Head on over to the palace and say, "Move on over, Saul. There's a new king in town"?

Sure. He could have. But then again, he was only about fifteen. And his only experience was tending sheep and schlepping lunch for his older brothers. Who was going to believe that God had selected a red-faced adolescent kid from the back valley to be king?

Sure. Filled with the bravado of his new calling, he could have rushed ahead. But instead, he went back to the valley and tended his sheep.

And he waited. For about fifteen years.

But he was active while he waited. He killed a bear, a lion, and other predators that threatened his flock. Maybe he slayed a giant or two. He went about his business and waited for God's timing. When it was time, he replaced Saul as the king of Israel.

Remember Esther? She also waited a long time, in a terrible set of circumstances, before God revealed his purpose for her. If she'd tried to take matters into her own hands, in her own time, the outcome would have looked different.

There is an important process from anointing to appointing.

Just because David had a call and had great gifts didn't mean it was time to throw Saul out and announce there was a new king in town. He had to go back to tending his sheep and tending his soul.

He had to develop into a great man of God.

He had to develop the character that was needed to do the work he was called to do in the future.

The same was true of Esther.

And the same is true for you.

As you read these words, did the dream inside you come to mind? Or maybe you found yourself getting frustrated all over again that God's timeline doesn't match your own. Or maybe you're confused because God gave you a gift but you're still stuck on the sidelines waiting to use it.

I hear you.

And most importantly, God hears you. He knows. He is with you every step of the way. He has you in the messy middle for a reason. He is actively putting all the puzzle pieces together for you.

You are growing to be the great woman of God you've always been destined to be.

Our goals and dreams often take longer to materialize than we would prefer. In those seasons, we gain skills, experience, and wisdom that will propel us into the next season.

The world needs women who will walk faithfully and fearlessly in their gifts, not to glorify the gifts but to bring glory to God. You were created to partner with God by bringing his purposes to life in this world. You and I were created to be great women of God and to do the work of God right here, right where we are.

God prepares us for what he has for us, one layer at a time. You haven't been given your gifts by accident. Guard your vision, make sure the soundtrack of the messy middle is one that encourages you and reminds you of the truth, work hard, get your reps in, and let him strengthen you for the future he laid out for you before the creation of the world.

You are an *ezer*, a helper, a completer, an answer to problems. You are stronger than you know because God is within you. Trust the process and walk out of the no-man's-land of the messy middle like the strong woman you are.

I Want You to Remember

Waiting doesn't mean allowing ourselves to be paralyzed with fear and doubt; it means moving forward (yes, even in those single, scared, shaking steps) in courage to build our strength.

God won't do for you the tasks he has given you to do.

Ain't nothin' holy about giving up when God calls you to get strong.

The waiting, the in-between, the messy middle is where the good and the hard stuff is. This is where your wobbly legs get strong, where the voice you've lost comes back. It's where the heart that was broken gets healed.

The world needs women who will walk faithfully and fearlessly in their gifts.

Discussion Questions

1. Belief is a choice. What are you currently choosing to believe about God, yourself, your circumstances, and others?
2. Is it easier to believe good things for others than for yourself? If so, why?
3. In what areas do you sense God is strengthening you?

Action Steps

Prayer: Read Isaiah 40:31. Ask God to raise your expectations.

Journal: Testimonies build our faith and remind us that breakthroughs can come from seasons of waiting. Take time to remember your stories of God's breakthroughs. Write them down so you can bring them out in hard seasons and ask God to "Do It Again."

Practice: Make worship your weapon. Next time you feel stuck, turn on your favorite worship playlist and sing songs of truth over your situation.

Fourteen

Show Up as You Really Are

This Is Me

The question comes at least once a week.

"Mom," my middle schoolers say, "why do you have to be so extra?"

By "extra," they mean over-the-top, excessive, too much. They think I'm extra. Friend, never let teenagers be the source of your daily affirmation. They can be brutal.

But I have to admit, my kids aren't all that wrong. After all, I was the nerdy twelve-year-old who loved self-help books, the stay-at-home mom turned accidental entrepreneur, and the businesswoman who closed up shop to help build a ministry. In every stage of my life, I've always felt weird, a little bit off, over the top, too much, *extra*.

As I look back now, I can clearly see that when I was in the role of an executive, I tucked much of my personality into my pocket when I showed up for work. And I shelved the "real Alli" when I showed up online because my online presence was a reflection of the organization. Taking the role of COO, knowing I had never run an organization as an executive before, I didn't want to be "extra" Alli. I wanted to be professional, executive material—whatever that meant. I had run my company, but it was my own and that felt loosey-goosey to me. In my mind, being a COO was serious business.

Being the ever-resourceful researcher, I researched. I googled. I bought as many books as I could find on how to be a good boss and team player, how to work well in an organizational structure, and even how to make sure I would be a good employee.

A year into my role, feeling pretty confident that I was killing it, I had coffee with a friend. She asked, "Alli, what's going on? I see you collapsing in on yourself here."

She said she saw me losing myself, losing what made me, me.

"It's like you are afraid of letting anyone down or doing the wrong thing. You're shrinking. *Where are you?*"

She wasn't wrong. I was shrinking away. I thought that was what I was supposed to do; I assumed that this was just my life now—that I had to show up in a certain way to be accepted, all the while tucking away the part of me that was, well, *extra.*

I felt my calling held the tension that I was to be what was needed while abandoning what I really wanted. I missed being myself, not only my extra self but also the person I was before I became "Alli Worthington, Executive."

My prayers in the early days of the role revolved around these themes: Lord, don't let me mess this up. I feel like I'm going crazy because I left my company. I'm trying to do a good job here, and I want to do a great job with the honor of helping to build this, but it's a lot all of a sudden. Help me not be sad about the life I've left behind (being an entrepreneur, getting to be freer and more creative). What are you doing with my life? What happened to my other dreams? Am I missing something? Help me not mess this up.

Just a few months into my role, the team I worked with went to Greece. At breakfast on day two, we were told that our evening worship would be a night of prophecy, and if we had anything to confess, we better take it to Jesus before tonight if we didn't want everyone to know it.

What?

Panic set in.

My Southern Baptist roots run deep. I went to a Southern Baptist school, and I'm the granddaughter of a Southern Baptist preacher. I wasn't sure what a night of prophecy meant, but it didn't sound good. I returned to my hotel room, dropped to my knees, and in a panicked fury confessed everything I could think of. I repented for stuff I for sure had done, things I wasn't sure if I did, and things I probably had done but couldn't remember for sure. I wasn't taking any chances.

I had no need for someone to announce all my sinful thoughts and weaknesses to a crowded room. "This is a disaster!" my conscience screamed. All day I walked around smiling, trying to seem calm, while inside I felt like all my dark-hearted secrets were about to be unearthed in a cosmic, spiritual truth-or-dare.

When the sun disappeared, we all met in a building on a busy square in Thessaloniki. As I climbed three flights of dark, cramped stairs, my panic turned to anticipation. I felt something stir inside me. What was God going to do? Was he really in this? Was this how he worked sometimes? If so, I wanted more of him. And if more of him meant letting go of anything I'd held on to, I was ready for that too.

I told God that if he was in this, then I was in. Whatever he had for me, I wanted it, and I didn't care what the consequences were. I was here for it.

Upon entering the meeting, we were told that we could relax. It was going to be a life-giving prophecy, which was a new phrase for me. No one was being called out; that wasn't how it worked. I didn't know whether to laugh or be angry, but I could breathe again.

A special guest arrived to share prophetically with us. I half expected her to look like a gypsy fortune-teller, but she looked like neither. Havilah looked like a mom who probably shopped at Target just like me. She was a mom of four boys and was from a small town in California.

What happened that night taught me never to put God in a box or assume I know how he works.

We stood up one by one, and this woman, a stranger to me, spoke about what she felt like God was telling her. Item by item she named truths she couldn't have known. As my turn came closer, I felt a mixture of excitement, terror, and intrigue. Would she really hear something from God to tell me? Is this possible? Maybe in Bible days. Does God do that now? If so, how did I not know about this? Why didn't this happen at my church?

My turn came. A colleague had the good sense to record on her phone what came next. Havilah said,

You are a unique woman. A triple threat. You are ministry, marketplace, and CEO. You have been made an expert in many fields, but you have felt like you are going crazy wondering what God is going to do with the gifts he put in you. You've wondered if you are missing something.

You need to hear this. You're right on the timeline that God has for you.

You're not going to miss what God has for you.

Sometimes musical notes are played in a seemingly chaotic way. The notes and instruments haven't been arranged yet. There's a perfect timing when your gift mix is going to come together, when it all comes together and all the instruments are played at just the right moment.

They've all been there since you were a little girl. You asked, "God, what are you going to do with all this?"

> Don't let the enemy lie to you that you are going mess this up. You are not going to mess this up. You are perfect for the job.
>
> You are going to get out of the boat, and you are not going to sink. You are not going to sink.
>
> Walk through those waters.
>
> You've let things die and said, "Lord, I don't know how this is going to work out," and the Lord said, "I'm going to bring it all back. I'm going to bring it all back to you."

I stood and shook as she spoke. God chose that day to tell me everything I needed to hear to keep going. Tears streamed down my face, and I didn't even care who saw. God was so gracious to use the words of a stranger to tell me I was on the right path and I needed to stand strong and walk it out.

I lived thirty years of my life before I experienced God speaking to me the first time, and when I was thirty-eight, he let me experience him speaking so clearly and with such detail through someone else. I was shocked. I didn't have the theology to support what I experienced, but I watched her interact similarly with everyone she spoke to. I felt a mix of humility and excitement, overwhelmed by this God I didn't know. There was so much I hadn't scratched the surface of before.

Three days later I flew home and couldn't wait to tell Mark everything: ". . . and then she said this. And then my whole body felt like I was freezing, but I was also hot on the inside. It was amazing and terrible and incredible all at once. So . . . what do you think?"

I had woken him up for this life-altering conversation. He listened groggily but intently, nodded, and said, "Well, that sounds amazing and pretty wild." (Mark, bless him, he's a man of few words.) I looked at the whole experience as God graciously letting me know I was meant for the job, I wasn't going to mess everything up, and to keep on going. That was that. Cool experience. End of story.

Years passed and life got harder. You know what happened in those years. Mark got sick, I got sick, and life was a mix of wonderful and heartbreaking depending on the day. The wild experience and the impact of that prophecy were eventually pushed aside as my day-to-day charged on.

Symphony Season

After that trip, I finally hit my stride in my new role. I finally felt needed; I finally felt and believed my work was meaningful. Fast-forward three years: I was still adjusting to the idea of going out into the unknown without a safety net. And as I continued to come to terms with my fear that God wouldn't keep his promises to me, a new thought crept in.

If I'm not in this role anymore, who will I be?

After I'd been an executive for almost four years, what would others need from me now? How was I going to show up? I knew my roles as wife and mother would remain unchanged. But without a professional role, I wasn't sure how the world would need me and who I needed to be.

In a world where people are supposed to create an all-encompassing and consistent "brand" for themselves, I was a weirdo. I had a public life as an author, I was preparing to launch a podcast, and I was rebuilding my coaching business.

When people previously asked what I did, my answer was tidy. Now when people asked, "What are you going to be doing?" I stammered and stuttered and threw out the world's worst run-on sentences. "I'll be writing books still and also I'm thinking about launching a podcast and bringing Blissdom back, maybe building something new for aspiring writers and also coaching women in business but not only women who run their own business but also women who are already in their career job and want to move to the next level and other stuff like that."

Other stuff like that. Clearly I had it together.

Although my answers weren't neat and tidy, I clung to two truths: God had called and equipped me to preach and to coach women.

When I told my *former* speaking agency that I was ready to fill my calendar and wanted to serve both ministries and business events, I was told that businesses wouldn't want me because I wrote books about Jesus. "Alli, you can't get corporate events to book you anymore. You're too controversial," my agent said. "Corporate event planners will see you write Christian books, and it's not a chance they want to take. No one lives in the world of business and faith. Pick one and focus on it."

Women who talk about Jesus can't talk about business, apparently.

This woman did.

Once again I was the weird girl who didn't quite fit in. Insecurity and anxiety over what I was doing were heavy weights that I kept picking back up and carrying around.

In the middle of all this, right before I left my job, a friend gifted Mark and me with tickets to a Christmas concert in Nashville, and we dressed up for a fancy and free night out together. It was a welcome distraction. I was still stressing and obsessing about our financial security and my health. If I had a moment to sit still, my mind would quickly wander to those insecurities. Even in the middle of the concert, I began obsessing.

As I was half listening to the concert and half running through my normal list of fears—would my voice ever come back, could I support our family, would Mark stay in remission—God broke through my brooding thoughts and said, "Symphony season." I looked around at the ornate room that held the concert. It was the local symphony hall, after all. I thought, "Symphony season. Okay, I guess people go to the symphony a lot this time of year. Cool."

Again he spoke. *Your symphony season is coming.* And he brought to mind the words from almost four years before.

There's a perfect timing when your gift mix is going to come together, when it all comes together and all the instruments are played at just the right moment.

God wanted me to know I was headed into a symphony season where my gift mix would play beautifully together. The notes that felt like they were a jumbled mess, that were playing discordant music, were falling in line, and the music would be beautiful.

I was not to fear that he created me to serve both ministry and business. I would not play the game of "this is spiritual and better" and this is "secular and not important." It was all important, and *it all mattered to God.*

Sometimes we think the way he created us is flawed, that if we are drawn to disparate callings, we are weird, that not acting like everyone around us is a sign of unhealth.

What if what we call weird is a symphony of notes placed perfectly by our Maker, which at the perfect moment falls in line and becomes beautiful music?

The words that surrounded me in an ancient room in Thessaloniki, Greece, were sent back to me as a beacon of hope to remind me that God was in control, he hadn't forgotten me, and he could be trusted to keep his promises.

Step out of the boat; walk on the water. Take my hand; you won't sink. I've got you.

There I was in a gorgeous symphony hall, ordained by God to be there, gifted with tickets to go so he could remind me he was still in control. I may be weird, but it was exactly how he created me. He created me on purpose, with a purpose.

Sometimes we feel like our weirdness, our gift mix, or our personalities are flawed, don't we? As if there is a "right" way to do things and somehow in our DNA we missed the memo when we were being formed. Somehow we don't add up. We're weird. Wrong. Lacking.

It reminds me of my friend Meredith, who was an incredible businesswoman. At only twenty-four years of age, she had been promoted from receptionist to purchasing manager to branch manager of one of the largest uniform rental companies in the country. By twenty-six she had given birth to two children, and she and her husband were both climbing the corporate ladder at a breathtaking pace.

Then one day, as she was picking up her sons from daycare, she had this overwhelming feeling she was supposed to quit her job and stay at home full-time with her children. Financially, it didn't make sense. But that's not the part that worried her. If she quit her job, it would be career suicide. If she ever decided to go back to work, she'd have to start all over.

But she knew leaving was what God was calling her to do, and she felt confident.

Those first few weeks at home, she was delighted to be living in her new calling. She whipped her house into an organizational masterpiece. Her kids were on a schedule that would have impressed even the busiest CEO. Then one day she ran into an old friend who asked, "What are you doing these days?" And Meredith answered, "Oh, I'm *just* staying at home with the kids."

It struck without warning. That feeling of self-doubt. Who was she now? She went from leading a multimillion-dollar company to making play dates for toddlers. What was she contributing to the world? To her family's finances? Did she even matter anymore?

Of course everyone else could answer those questions for her. She was living out God's unique calling for her to stay at home and raise her children. But all she could hear was self-doubt.

The enemy wields self-doubt like a weapon to injure us, destroy us, or even just distract us from our callings. It's easier to believe we are too weird or too unremarkable, too uneducated or too cerebral, too messy or too inexperienced, too young or too old, too important or too insignificant to accomplish what God has placed in our hearts.

WE CAN FIND THE CONFIDENCE TO SHOW UP EVEN WHEN WE FEEL LESS-THAN, BECAUSE WE SERVE A GOD WHO IS MORE-THAN.

What would happen if a generation of women committed to overcoming their self-doubt and showing up for the life God placed them in, no matter how different or how lacking they felt?

Instead of hiding our gifts, we would share them with people who need them. Instead of questioning why we are the way we are, we could trust the God who knit us together in our mothers' wombs. Instead of allowing ourselves to wallow in insecurity, we could step forward in confidence.

We can't let self-doubt steal our faith and script our future.

We can find the confidence to show up even when we feel less-than, because we serve a God who is more-than. He brings healing, redemption, strength, and confidence.

Show up broken; he'll make you whole.
Show up weird; he'll use it for his glory.
Show up when everything in you tells you to shrink back;
    he'll make you strong.
Show up with your jumbled gifts; he'll arrange a symphony.

The Silent Epidemic

I fell in love with the internet and social media twelve years ago. I am part of a pioneering generation of women who first harnessed the power of the web to learn whatever we wanted to learn and build businesses online from our living rooms with kids at our feet. Women, for the first time in history, didn't need anyone's approval or permission to learn, create, and build anything we could dream.

And now I love helping women from all over the world build their businesses, nonprofits, writing and speaking careers, and ministries. As a coach, I get to help businesswomen manage their teams, be effective and kind leaders, balance their work and family life, and I even help with spiritual development. I love the women I work with, and over time, they begin to feel like family.

I may be unusual, walking between the world of business and ministry every day, but the music fits me just fine.

What I've learned through the years is that it's not my job to try to make everyone accept who I was created to be. And it's not my job to try to create a version of myself that makes sense to others. My job is to step out, show up, and be who God made me to be. Nothing more, nothing less.

Comparison: The Calling Killer

The freedom the internet offers us is good and powerful.

Yet I have lived on it long enough to see social media go from being a place of connection to a place cluttered with filtered, curated, perfected versions of people who don't exist. We show up for everyone, but we don't show anyone who we really are.

The problem is that we can't help but compare our real life with everyone's highlights.

This hurts because we diminish our confidence to show up. Comparison is a silent epidemic that feeds the twin fires of self-doubt and playing small, both of which threaten to snuff out our dreams.

Digital comparison suffocates our willingness to step out and show up.

We see someone else doing something we want to try.

We tell ourselves it has already been done and so we won't try.

We see someone else posting picture-perfect photos that look like they must have a camera crew and makeup artist following them around every day.

We tell ourselves that no one wants to see our real lives anyway.

We see someone living what seems to be a perfect life.

We tell ourselves we are destined to live in lack.

But here is what I know from coaching women through the years: every woman struggles.

You never know what goes on behind closed doors, no matter how someone's life looks on social media. Insecurity runs rampant in the hearts of women of all ages, socioeconomic statuses, colors, shapes, and sizes. No one is immune, no matter how their perfectly put-together, carefully curated life appears on social media.

Comparing your life to curated content is a calling killer.

It's a calling killer because we compare and we shrink, we compare and we doubt ourselves, we compare and we hold back. We compare and we take our eyes off what God wants us to do, instead focusing on closing the gap between where we know we are going and where we are now.

Let's be women who know the dangers of social media–fueled comparison and intentionally use social media for good. Let's use our online presence as the light-bearers we are. Use it for good; call out good in others, cheer on your friends, and post what builds others up. Be you, show up, don't shrink back, and don't play small.

When you, created by God for greatness, play small, the entire world misses out. Use your voice for good.

Let's redeem what can be toxic. Let's make our little corners of the internet world be those known for grace, inclusion, and love.

Jesus didn't die on the cross simply to let social media steal the lives he has prepared for us. He didn't save us from hell so we could beat ourselves up with the club of comparison. Being who we are, where we are, can complete the work he has given us in this season.

It's our job to show up and change the world by sharing our gifts and serving those God puts in our paths.

You were born at this time in history for a reason. You were given your exact mix of gifts, strengths,

> JESUS DIDN'T SAVE US FROM HELL FOR US TO BEAT OURSELVES UP WITH THE CLUB OF COMPARISON.

weaknesses, quirks, habits, and personality for a reason. It's no accident your feet are planted exactly where they are today.

Just like Esther trusted the greatness of the God she served even though she didn't know what greatness God had planned for her, you may not have all the answers, but know that God has your back.

You are on a mission, great woman of God.

Kill comparison before it kills your call.

Your mix of gifts is unique to you.

Your symphony will play a tune all your own.

Your calling won't look like anyone else's, ever.

Here's what I know for sure: God chose you. He made you exactly who you are. He set your life in motion. He put you here on earth right here, right now, because he wants you to partner with him, and he has something special that only you can do in his kingdom.

God wants to use everything you think is weird about yourself. He wants to take everything bad that has happened to you and redeem it for his glory.

SOMETHING SPECIFIC NEEDS TO BE DONE IN THE KINGDOM, AND ONLY YOU CAN DO IT.

Let's be women who decide to bring all of ourselves to the table.

Let's be women who don't let our pasts define our futures.

Let's be women whom life may kick around sometimes, but who get back up and keep going.

Let's be women who live with open hands for what God has for us.

Let's be women who stand strong and change the world, who work for the kingdom, doing God's work around us, right where we are.

We need to show up for ourselves, for our daughters, for the women who come after us.

We have to stop playing small; we have to stop letting fear sideline us.

Let's cheer each other on, though we show up weak but ready to be made strong.

God has orchestrated a symphony just for you, and it's a beautiful sound. He's asking you to keep showing up and enjoy the music.

I Want You to Remember

We have to show up even when we feel less-than, because we serve a God who is more-than.

Comparison is a silent epidemic that feeds the twin fires of self-doubt and playing small, both of which threaten to snuff out our dreams.

Let's be women who know the dangers of social media–fueled comparison but choose to redeem what can be toxic. Let's make our little corners of the internet world be those known for grace, inclusion, and love.

Jesus didn't die on the cross simply to let social media steal the lives he has prepared for us.

God put you here on earth right here, right now, because he wants you to partner with him, and he has something special that only you can do in his kingdom.

Discussion Questions

1. In the age of social media, it's easier than ever before to compare everything about our lives, including our callings. Have you compared your calling with someone else's?
2. Is comparison killing your willingness to step out and show up?
3. What is your "symphony" of talents and interests?

Action Steps

Prayer: Ask God to show you who you are and reveal how he wants to use you, in your uniqueness, to accomplish his plans.

Journal: Instead of focusing on what you or others think is "wrong" with you (too much, too quiet, too perfect), make a list of what is right with you. Invite God to partner with you in this exercise since it can sometimes be a struggle to think well of ourselves. Do any of the things you listed surprise you? What on this list jumps out at you? Does the world around you get to experience your amazing-ness? If not, it's time to show up and let God show you off.

Practice: Use your online presence to be a light-bearer. Use it for good; call out good in others, cheer on your friends, and post what builds others up. Be you, show up, don't shrink back, and don't play small. Use your voice for good.

Fifteen

Find Your Strength in Community

I've Got All My Sisters with Me

My mom picked me up from my Montessori preschool and found me in a dramatic, nearly hysterical state. Unable to get much more from me than sobs, she honed in on the one complete sentence I could choke out. "They got in a circle and spit on me!"

My mother marched up to the teacher's desk to find out exactly what was going on.

"Alli has lots of friends," my teacher said. "She and the other girls get along well. I can assure you *no one* formed a circle around her and spit on her."

Mom couldn't decide if I was being dramatic over some small slight at the sandbox or if it really did happen the way I described it. Did Jennie pick Hayley over me for kickball? And did I just *feel* unloved and unwanted, or did Jennie and Hayley and their posse of preschool thugs *truly* have it in for me at the playground?

At this point, even *I* can't remember what went on back in preschool, but what I do know is that from my earliest days, I longed for friends.

The girls at my private middle school always made fun of me—the poor girl, the girl who was so excited about getting carpet in her bedroom. Never once throughout my adolescence did I take a chance and have a friend over. I kept girls at arm's length because of the secret shame of my shack of a barn home, the symbol of my poverty.

This only continued as I grew older. In college I quit my sorority because my insecurities told me I'd never measure up. I was too tall, too poor, too wide, and too weird to be in their sisterhood. So I left, which, at the time, felt like a better option than sticking around and waiting for my inadequacies to come to light.

It's not that I didn't long for sisterhood; I just didn't think I'd ever truly have it. Even after passing through the awkwardness of adolescence and young adulthood, I still struggled to build deep friendships. And our family moved every two years for the first ten years of my married life, so making and keeping girlfriends was unattainable . . . impossible.

And then I found a sisterhood in the most unexpected of places—online. Those in my online community became some of my dearest friends, one of the only constants when my life—and address—was ever changing. But even so, I often convinced myself that these women were my online friends only because they didn't know me in real life.

But isn't it just like God to take the wounds we consider weaknesses and turn them into great gifts for the kingdom? I was an only child, and I had only sons. I didn't have many girlfriends growing up. In my mind, I didn't measure up, and that left me feeling a bit odd. So what do I do with my life? God orchestrated it that I would devote it to investing in women.

Life rarely makes sense while we are living it. It only makes sense when we can look back and connect the dots. In the moment, the dots seem erratic and spread wild. But when time gives us the distance to peer over our shoulders, we catch a glimpse of the masterpiece that God has been crafting with our lives since the beginning.

For Our Good, for His Glory

Helping women grow, succeed, and find confidence has been at the heart of my work for over a decade. Two sectors that I once assumed were opposing forces—business and ministry—I now recognize as complementary pieces in God's grand design. I marvel at how God took the crying outcast girl and made her life's work about gathering and empowering women.

What the world says is impossible, what we believe is impossible, God makes possible.

My mentor in high school told me that God redeems every part of our lives for our good and for his glory. During seasons when I felt like I was walking through hell, I didn't find much comfort in that truth. But with a little distance, I've been able to look back and see that God *does* redeem every part of our lives—for our good and for his glory.

Those of us who have traversed down the shadowy valley of life are expertly equipped to help others travel to the mountaintop. God takes every wound, every story of suffering, and every weakness and transforms them into tools for healing and hope, goodness and glory.

My childhood wounds were numerous—a father who died too soon, a barn-bound existence, the terror of childhood bullies—but God took the raw materials of those weaknesses and fashioned them to be my greatest strengths.

This is how the Cosmic Craftsman works, how our God makes miracles.

Maybe you're not great with adults, but you love kids. That's not a weakness. It's what makes you such a great teacher or mom or pediatrician. Perhaps you've never really enjoyed working for someone else. That's not a weakness. God gave you a desire to work for yourself and the creativity to go with it. Maybe you aren't great at in-depth conversations. That's not a weakness. Your ability to make small talk sets people at ease in new situations.

I loved to hibernate and read as a kid. Information feeds my soul. The enemy convinced me I was weird, a book nerd, and an introvert who had no friends. But God gave me a love for research that would someday allow me to help women find their callings in different seasons of life.

I love to see women find deep, abiding friendships in life, but the enemy convinced me I'd never have friends like that. I have a quirky, fun-loving personality, but the enemy told me that my introverted self was boring and awkward.

Everything I have ever considered a weakness, and everything I have walked through—from the tragedies of death, illness, and poverty to everyday trials including starting a business, raising sons, and navigating broken relationships—has become a valuable tool in God's kingdom renovation project.

When your calling is to build up and speak into the lives of women, people want to talk to someone they can relate to, someone who has "been there." Not only have I been there, but I still have days when life knocks me around and the enemy jumps in to remind me that I don't have it all together. I'm a great coach, but that doesn't mean I don't need someone to walk with me through the valleys from time to time.

You can't lead people through dark days if you haven't battled through them yourself a time or two. **When a woman has walked through what feels like hell, she can show her sisters how to stand strong too.**

Standing strong happens in community.

Strengthened in Community

My community of women, some of whom live in my town, some of whom live across the country, is what helped me learn to stand strong through my seasons of struggle and self-doubt.

This group included the women in my weekly Bible study who encouraged me when I would cry and say, "I'm obeying, but I sure hope God shows up." The women who laid hands on me when I would show up with my mug of hot tea and couldn't share because if I talked, a coughing attack would start. The women who stepped out in faith and delivered messages from the Lord to me, not knowing how I would respond. The women who answered my self-pitying texts with grace and optimism when it would have been so easy to tell me to get a hold of myself.

It is often taught that we heal in community. And friendships are often Jesus's favorite way to bring us into wholeness, into a new season of strength, and into new wisdom.

Jesus modeled community for us in the most beautiful ways. His close friendships involved people from every walk of life: from Peter, who had no impulse control; to Thomas, who overthought everything; to Martha, the worrier, and Mary, the worshiper; to Matthew, the tax collector. Jesus built community with people who were different from him.

From this cast of seeming misfits, God provided people to walk with Jesus on earth through what would be his hardest days. And in that crazy community, the only common denominator being Jesus, they all found healing, forgiveness, and joy. They found friendships that would carry them through the highest of highs and the lowest of lows.

If my closest girlfriends weren't women who loved the Lord, who would have reminded me that he who calls us is faithful to complete us? If my friends weren't women devoted to prayer, who would have heard him whisper to send me a message to stop staying stuck in fear and to step out of the boat in faith? If my friends weren't women who prioritize being loving and present even when their friend isn't fun to be around because of illness, grief, or depression, who would have been there when my strength wavered? If my friends hadn't earned my respect and trust all these years, how would I have known whose counsel to trust?

It is in community that we find a support system and a sacred sisterhood. When a group of women come together, standing strong in the gifts God has given them, there's no stopping them. That's what was so special about Blissdom—the sisterhood, the community.

Bringing Blissdom back in the fall of 2019 was like winning the Super Bowl and a Nobel Prize all in the same day. It was everything I wanted it to be and more. God was so gracious to allow me to bring it back. I was in my sweet spot once again, running a conference for women entrepreneurs. The event felt full circle—me obeying and shutting it down, growing up for a few years, and getting to bring it back better than ever. I was overjoyed.

After the closing session, I held a reception in my suite to celebrate the success. I hugged everyone goodbye, then ran myself a long-deserved bath. As I slipped down into the water, I breathed a contented sigh and thanked God, once again, for the opportunity.

In that moment I heard God say in my spirit, "Do not plan for next year." I sat up so quickly, the water sloshed over the edges of the tub. NO WAY! Surely, I had not heard him correctly. Surely, I was not going to be the girl who had to quit, again.

For weeks I prayed, hoping that somehow it was my fear talking to me and God would break through and tell me it was all in my head. I needed it to be all in my head. I needed it not to be true. No matter how hard I tried not to hear it, he remained clear that it wasn't happening in 2020.

I was angry at God for allowing me to bring something back and then telling me to stop it again. I just didn't understand. None of it made sense. It was successful. The women had loved it. I dreaded going back to my partners, yet again, to tell them that Blissdom would not come back next year.

But even though I was angry and confused and embarrassed at the thought that I was, once again, the girl who quit inexplicably, I still obeyed. If I had learned anything through this season, it was that blessing follows obedience.

I didn't know we couldn't gather again in 2020, but God did.

I didn't know a pandemic was coming in 2020, but God did.

Before the pandemic started, after I grieved the loss of Blissdom (*again!*) I began dreaming a new dream to gather women in community online in an intentional way. I wanted to use technology to build an online coaching community where women could come together and support each other's dreams and callings. Now, more than ever, community is a lifeline. Video calls, group video chats, and apps that make connection easy are important now more than ever before. We have learned that friendships that span across cities, states, and countries are just as real, important, and necessary as those in our physical space. Technology isn't just a blessing for community; it's the best thing for community—both in real life and online.

With my friend Lisa, I cofounded Called Creatives, a coaching community for women who feel called to write and speak. Too many women shrink back from this calling because of self-doubt and the lies of the enemy. Called Creatives provides training and equipping so members can write their books and learn to share messages and tell their stories with confidence. It has been such a joy to see this community of women supporting each other, sharing their wisdom and tips, and cheering each other on as we run hard after God's call in our lives.

In community, we are strengthened to fulfill our callings in each season. We are taught, counseled, encouraged, warned, and loved by our community. Something powerful happens when women share their stories, whether it's with each other or with a broken world.

The enemy wants us to ignore our callings, to stay stuck, silent, and frozen in self-doubt. But our sacred sisters won't let that happen. That's why we need them.

My season of struggle, self-doubt, and losing confidence in myself and God is a crazy topic for a book. The behind-the-scenes of a crisis in my life that only God, my husband, and a few close friends knew about, I now share here in painstaking detail because my story is a love letter to God. It's a letter of gratitude for my community, the women I call my friends. And it's a goodbye to self-doubt and lack of confidence, the tools the enemy tried to use to take me out.

Your Invitation

My good, bad, and ugly are all here for you because, like my friends who wiped my tears, who reminded me to get back up, who spoke of God's goodness when I was spiraling downward, I pray I can be a voice for you. My prayer is that I'm one of those voices in your life that is encouraging, that I remind you to remember what God has for you, to not hold yourself back, and to keep walking strong into that future he has crafted for you.

I have prayed for you. I have prayed that the message in this book in your hands will be deeply instilled within you—that as you learn about the struggle in my story, you lean into the strength of your own.

You are invited to see your messy, mundane, hard, wonderful journey for what it is: a calling to confidently step into your season with strength.

God has embedded gifts and talents in you that are waiting to be discovered. They are no longer discordant notes trying to find somewhere to land; they are falling into place to create beautiful music.

And God is inviting both you and me into his song, into his symphony.

God has invested too much in you for you to let the enemy hold you back.

The enemy will try to take you out. He can't steal you from God's hand, but he will work overtime to keep you distracted, depressed, and disillusioned. Jesus won the war on Calvary, but you, sister, you are in a battle every day.

The enemy will tell you that your calling doesn't match your credentials, but God is a God of empowerment. The enemy will tell you that the world has changed and your dreams no longer matter, but God is not surprised by world events, and your calling remains for you to live it out. The enemy will tell you that you are weak, but God reminds us that the Holy Spirit in us is bigger than any giants in front of us. The enemy will tell you that you have to always be who you were, but God whispers that you are a new creation and his grace is enough. The enemy will throw hell at you to convince you to sideline yourself, but God calls you to get in the game. The enemy will tell you that you should hold back, but God invites you to stop playing small. The enemy will lie to you that stepping out is prideful, but God asks you to be bold and humble with confidence from him.

Keep doing your kingdom work, keep dreaming, keep listening to the dream you have in your heart, and know God placed it there as a vision for the future he has for you.

God is waiting for you with open hands, asking you to partner with him as you bring his plans to life.

Many people who are less qualified than you are doing what you dream of doing because they decided to trust God instead of staying in the doldrums of doubt.

The Bible is filled with stories of people who chose to step out beyond qualification.

Moses was a fugitive, not a prophet.

Noah was a winemaker, not a shipbuilder.

Esther was a concubine, not a truth-teller.

David was a shepherd, not a giant slayer.

Gideon was a farmer, not a military operative.

Rahab was a harlot, not a spy.

Nehemiah was a butler, not an urban planner.

My real-talk translation: Stop telling God what you can't do. Stop telling God why you aren't good enough. Stop telling God *no* through your actions. Step up, step out, love big, let it all be messy and imperfect, and trust God's goodness and his grace, even when life doesn't make sense.

Playing small is easy and safe. It feels good to use humility as a cover for disobedience. But God is asking a generation of women to stand strong, to listen to that whisper inside that says you are meant for more. Your symphony season is coming. Let him guide you, let him bring you through the seasons that stretch you, let him redeem your trials for your good and his glory, and share your story.

My prayer for you is that you continue to walk your journey with strength and grace, that you embrace the mantle of a great woman of God, that you live a life of service, love, bravery, and making peace with the temporary discomfort that comes along with growth.

STOP TELLING GOD WHAT YOU CAN'T DO.

I pray that you go *all in* for this next season of your life. I pray that God burns every bridge that could lead you back to the old you, who holds you back from the new you that you are and are becoming. Listen to the dreams God has planted in your heart, no matter how improbable they seem, how unworthy or unable you feel, or how impossible they sound. Take new territory, knowing that God, who created you, also calls you to greatness.

Send fear, self-doubt, and shame back to hell where they belong.

You are an *ezer*, a helper, a completer, an answer to problems. You were designed with purpose to create, complement, and complete. You are a wonder, woman. You are on the front line taking bullets for the people you love.

Stay close to Jesus, ask for a fresh filling of the Holy Spirit, ask God to protect your family and your friends, and ask God to send in reinforcements. Pray that women like Carol, Bianca, and Stephanie will remind you that God is good, can be trusted, and will see you through.

God's heart for us is to accomplish extraordinary plans. He knows his call for us, an unknown future that will stretch us. It will require faith and courage and an all-out war on self-doubt. But the good news is that the God who calls us is faithful.

He is fierce.

He finds us worthy.

And he won't ever fail or forsake us.

So stand strong, sister. Take those shaky first steps forward. Invest in yourself, love big no matter how you've been hurt in the past, and serve the world around you. You were born for such a time as this.

You have what it takes because God lives inside you.

Keep standing strong, great woman of God, because he is faithful.

I Want You to Remember

God takes every wound, every pain, every suffering, and every weakness and transforms them into tools for healing and hope, goodness and glory.

God has invested too much in you for you to let the enemy hold you back.

Stop telling God what you can't do.

Pray that God burns every bridge that leads you back to the old you that holds you back. Listen to the dreams he has planted in your heart, no matter how improbable they seem, how unworthy or unable you feel, or how impossible they sound.

Send fear, self-doubt, and shame back to hell where they belong.

Discussion Questions

1. Are you currently cultivating community with others who can cheer you on in your God-given calling?
2. Do your current friendships drain you or strengthen you?
3. In what ways can you sow the kind of community you want to reap?

Action Steps

Prayer: Ask for a fresh filling of the Holy Spirit, ask God to protect your family and your friends, and ask God to send in reinforcements.

Journal: Review your past journal entries from your *Standing Strong* action steps. Take note of the revelations, the wins, and the growth you've already experienced by standing strong.

Practice: Use the notes from your time journaling through *Standing Strong* to identify three things you want to do in this season of life. Map out the investment of time and energy you want to make in your goals, and pray for a fresh filling of the Holy Spirit and God's strength and wisdom to partner with you every step of the way.

Acknowledgments

My Savior: Thank you, Jesus, for chasing me down when I tried to run, for rescuing me from myself, and for being more than everything I have ever hoped you would be. When I prayed, "What do you want me to say?" you answered, "Great woman of God," and left me to wrestle with that call and to find my answers in community. What an adventure this message has been in my life. Thank you for the honor of partnering with you to bring what I learned in this season to the world.

My family: Mark, you never doubt me, and you never tell me I shouldn't go for it. You always calmly look me in the eye when I tell you my next idea and say, "You'll do great!" and you mean it. I hope I never take for granted the support, love, and confidence you have in me. I couldn't do all that God has called me to do without your calm, loving, patient encouragement. I'm grateful I get to be your *ezer kenegdo*.

Justin, Jack, Joey, James, and Jeremiah, what a joy it is to be your mother. I love you with all my heart. I don't tell you enough how grateful I am for your support. You cheer me on and never hassle me for staying locked away in my office on a manuscript deadline. I'm so proud of each one of you. Just as I pray over you every night to become great men of God, I see each of you growing in strength, kindness, vision, discernment, and wisdom. It is the greatest happiness and thrill of my life to be your mother.

Mom, you are a great woman of God. Thank you for praying

that simple prayer over me, even in the years when it seemed like I would end up as anything but that. This message is here because you are a woman who wouldn't let life beat her down, who loved the Lord, and loved me and others fiercely. I love you so much.

Jessica, I'm so proud of the great woman of God you are becoming. I love you with all my heart.

My community: I've never felt so vulnerable writing a book before, and that says a lot given that my books are normally full of stories of how I messed things up and what I learned along the way. This book feels like I'm walking into a crowded room naked and announcing, "Here I am!" Because of the level of vulnerability and raw emotion I put into this, I've been lucky enough to have more help than ever before. So many people were kind enough to read, edit, and when asked, ruthlessly pick my words apart to make sure they would be clear, helpful, and most importantly, theologically sound.

Thank you, Carol, for your continued wisdom, your partnership, and your amazing ability to know what I meant to say. I'm so grateful God set us up as friends. Jonathan, when I asked you to "rip apart my words, and that I'm not precious with them," you believed me, and your brilliant guidance and honest critiques helped me write what was in my heart. Rachel, thank you for being a cover model and for that gorgeous manifesto that captures the essence of a woman standing strong so perfectly. Lindsay, your wisdom and practical guidance are a blessing! You are an amazing friend and cover model. Whitney, what a joy it is to work with you. Thanks for joining in and modeling for the cover. Shelby, you are the queen of catching inconsistencies! Amy, thank you for sharing your professional wisdom as a therapist and making sure my advice was helpful.

Jenna, I'm so thankful God put us in each other's lives. You are a friend who quickly became a sister. Thank you for always being on Team Alli for crazy adventures, movie marathons, and for sharing your wisdom and strategy. Two sevens really can change the world.

Jo, what would we do without our personal board of directors? I'm forever grateful for your friendship, your insight, and your strength. PBD forever!

Lisa, God is so good to take friends and make them cofounders. You are the perfect eight to my seven at Called Creatives. I'm so happy to get to lead with you. And thank you to the entire teams of Allison Worthington Media, Called Creatives, and Worthy Goods Co. What a joy it is to work alongside you to create products, trainings, and experiences to equip and encourage women to be all God has called them to be.

John Mark Comer, your work with Garden City opened my eyes to God's plan for our work. God used your work to spark mine. Thank you for your faithfulness to the message.

Christine Caine, thank you for the lessons. Thank you for the opportunity to build strength. And thank you for pushing me through the years.

My publishing team: Jenni, I'm so thankful for the brainstorming mental gymnastics we went through to get this vague "great woman of God" concept into practical steps for this project. Stephanie and the brilliant Zondervan team, thank you for your faith in me and my vision for this book since day one.

And last but not least, I'm thankful for you. Thank you for your support of my work. Thank you for sharing your heart with me via messages and coaching questions on my podcast. Thank you for leaving reviews on Amazon and iTunes. Thank you for sharing my work with your friends. Thank you for sending notes that gently ask me if I thought a certain statement through, because you don't want me to put my foot in my mouth. ☺

Thank you for supporting my family by purchasing my products, books, and trainings. I create it all for you. I literally could not do what I do without you, and I'm grateful to partner with you.

Notes

Chapter 3: Remember Who You Are

1. Robby Gallaty, "Message: 'A Woman Used by God' from Robby Gallaty," Long Hollow Baptist Church, February 9, 2020, https://longhollow.com/media/a-woman-used-by-god/.

Chapter 4: When You Forget Where Your Power Comes From

1. Yes, I know I'm skipping over the fall here, but I want to focus on our role as creators who rule over the earth. We're all way too familiar with the fall already; what we tend to skip over is our call to work, to create, and to build.

Chapter 8: When Insecurity and Doubt Are Loud

1. Mel Robbins, *The 5 Second Rule: Transform Your Life, Work, and Confidence with Everyday Courage* (Savio Republic, 2017).

Chapter 10: Ask for It

1. A. W. Tozer, "Why We Must Think Rightly About God," in *The Knowledge of the Holy* (New York: HarperCollins, 1978), 4.
2. Paul David Tripp, *New Morning Mercies: A Daily Gospel Devotional* (Wheaton, IL: Crossway, 2019), April 2.

Chapter 13: Trust the Process

1. John R. Kohlenberger, *NIV Exhaustive Bible Concordance*, 3rd ed. (Grand Rapids: Zondervan, 2015).
2. Albert Barnes, *Notes on the Old Testament: Job* (Grand Rapids: Baker, 2005).
3. Go to https://alliworthington.com/playlist to listen.

About Alli Worthington

Normally this is the place for a few paragraphs about the author, but at this point, I feel like we are old friends. What do you not know about me, right?

Good friends don't need introductions!

We've come a long way together, and I don't want our time to be over just because we've come to the end of the book.

On the next few pages, you'll find free gifts I have for you: a weekly devotional, my weekly show, and chapters from my books. You'll also find more ways we can connect and discover some of my work with Called Creatives and Worthy Goods Co. to equip and encourage women to stand strong. I would love for you to join me.

xo,

Alli

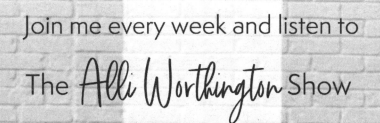

Join me every week and listen to

The *Alli Worthington* Show

I interview my friends and people
I look up to learn, laugh,
and have a great time.

I also answer your questions
about life, faith, and
business on every episode.

You can find the podcast on
your favorite podcast player.

AlliWorthington.com/Podcast

Free Friday Devotions

I would love to send a free devotion to you every Friday morning. They are short, power-packed, and created to help you stand strong.

AlliWorthington.com/Devotions

WORTHY
GOODS CO.

Worthy Goods Co. is a faith-based lifestyle brand that offers fun and inspiring apparel and accessories designed with you in mind. Through our line, we hope to be a spark that ignites meaningful conversations about life, love, and Jesus around the globe.

Whether you're running errands, building your career, or spending time with the ones you love, Worthy Goods Co. is there with you!

WorthyGoodsCo.com

You have to break the busy before the busy breaks you.

Breaking Busy marries research with solid biblical principles, giving you practical tools to move from crazy busy to confident calm. You'll learn the secrets to breaking out of a life of busyness, chaos, and stress. You'll discover how to overcome feeling a constant pressure to be all things to all people. *Breaking Busy* will give you the tools you need for self-care, relationships, boundaries, and time management. Join Alli and break the busy before the busy breaks you.

Download your free chapter at
AlliWorthington.com/BreakingBusy.

God didn't give you a spirit of fear; learn how to fight back against it.

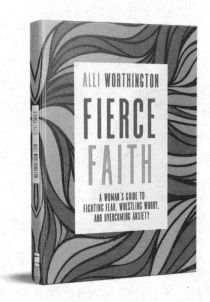

Fear, worry, anxiety—they don't have to keep you stuck anymore. Join Alli as she maps out common fears: betrayal, rejection, the fear of something happening to your children, failure, and fear of the future. You'll discover a customized battle plan for each fear, developed with research and biblical truth. You'll learn how to overcome negative thinking, overcome the big and little worries in life, and tackle a simple trick to stop the anxiety spiral.

Download your free chapter at
AlliWorthington.com/FierceFaith.

A devotional that brings practical tools and biblical truth together for greater joy and peace.

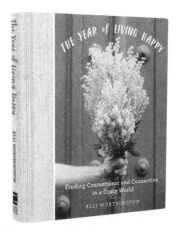

Filled with passages about what the Bible says brings happiness, with practical tools, and with lots of space to journal, this devotional will help you bring more joy to your everyday life. If you have ever wanted more happiness for your family, your friends, and your community, know that you can be the change that shifts the culture. Discover God's plan and what he says about happiness.

Download seven chapters free at
AlliWorthington.com/YearofLivingHappy.